CLASSIC ƒM

The *Friendly* Guide to

Elgar

Tim Lihoreau & Darren Henley

Hodder Arnold

www.hoddereducation.com

For UK order enquiries: please contact Bookpoint Ltd, 130 Milton Park, Abingdon, Oxon OX14 4SB. Telephone: +44(0) 1235 827720. Fax: +44(0) 1235 400454. Lines are open 09.00–18.00, Monday to Saturday, with a 24-hour message answering service. You can also order through our website www.hoddereducation.com

British Library Cataloguing in Publication Data: a catalogue record for this title is available from the British Library.

First published in UK 2007, by Hodder Education, 338 Euston Road, London NW1 3BH.

Typeset by Servis Filmsetting Ltd, Manchester
Printed in Great Britain for Hodder Education, a division of Hodder Headline, 338 Euston Road, London NW1 3BH, by Cox & Wyman Ltd, Reading, Berkshire.

Hodder Headline's policy is to use papers that are natural, renewable and recyclable products and made from wood grown in sustainable forests. The logging and manufacturing processes are expected to conform to the environmental regulations of the country of origin.

Impression number   10 9 8 7 6 5 4 3 2

Year   2011 2010 2009 2008 2007

"Music is in the air – you simply take as much of it as you want."

"Gosh, man, I've got a tune in my head."

Sir Edward Elgar

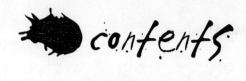

contents

Contents

Introduction

This book is for you whether you hail from
Scotland, Northern Ireland or Wales, or even from
further afield. But it is especially for you if you are
from England. It is a celebration of a man who
must surely rank as England's greatest composer and
whose music is regarded as the very epitome of
English country life.

These days it can sometimes be seen as
unfashionable to be thought of as being
quintessentially English. Yet Sir Edward Elgar
was as English as warm beer, cricket on the village
green or cucumber sandwiches with the crusts
chopped off.

His most popular hits, such as his *Cello Concerto,* always seem to be able to conjure up images in our minds of the rolling Malvern Hills around his beloved Worcestershire home. And then there are those great tunes written by Elgar that have come to be seen as almost eccentrically English. Where would any "Proms" concert, inside or out, up and down the country, be without the familiar strains of "*Land of Hope and Glory*"?

It is all too easy for Elgar's detractors to accuse him of writing music that merely plays to the lowest common denominator, stirring up those listening into a frenzy of jingoism. But he was no rabble-rouser. A thoughtful, intelligent, hard-working man, he was capable of writing tunes that connected with ordinary listeners. You can hum them while you're sitting at your computer or while you're behind the wheel of your car. They are memorable: sometimes fun; sometimes rumbustious; sometimes achingly beautiful; sometimes deeply melancholic. But this was a man who unfailingly knew how to write a great tune. And, we believe, that it was his ability as a tunesmith that enabled him to create music that continues to give all true Englishmen and Englishwomen that twinge of patriotism whenever they hear his work being played.

Just to stress the point, though, there isn't some sort of pre-programmed gene only present in those who were born in England that allows them to enjoy

Elgar's music. His creations have deservedly become popular the world over.

Sir Edward Elgar was a striking looking man, with a big bushy moustache. For many years, his was the face on the back of the English twenty-pound note. Apparently, such was the detail necessary to reproduce the appendage that sat nobly upon his top lip, that it made forgery very difficult for counterfeiters. Shockingly, the Bank of England saw fit to announce that they were removing his face from the notes just a year short of the 150th anniversary of the great man's birth, in 2007.

We should never underestimate the importance of Elgar in any history of English classical music. Before he came along, there had been an almost complete dearth of any great English composers. With the exception of Sir Arthur Sullivan, who was most famous for writing operettas, and Georg Frideric Handel, whom we "borrowed" from the Germans, we have to wind the clock back all the way to 1695, the year in which Henry Purcell died, to find another really significant Englishman who was writing music that has stood the test of time.

Well, Sir Edward Elgar put England and English music firmly back on the map. And for that alone, along with warm beer, cricket matches played on the village green and cucumber sandwiches with the crusts chopped off, we should cherish him.

As with the other *Friendly Guides* in this series, this book is not intended to bring new scholarly or musicological thinking to the life of our subject. Instead, this is the book about Elgar that is right for you, even if you wouldn't normally consider buying a book about classical music. These are the facts of his life, presented, we hope, in an engaging and enjoyable way.

Tim Lihoreau
Darren Henley
Classic FM, March 2007

A Friendly Word Before We Get Started . . .

As you might expect, this book contains many references to pieces of music. We wanted to make this guide to Elgar as friendly on the eye as possible, so we have decided to simplify the rules about how pieces of music appear:

- Titles of all musical works are set in italics.
- Songs and arias appear in italics within quotation marks.

Musical historians use "opus numbers" to help catalogue each composer's work.

To keep things as *friendly* as possible, we have only used opus numbers where it's necessary to include them so that we can avoid confusion between different works.

The Friendly Guide to What was Composed When

If you have ever visited London as a tourist, you may find that, after a while, you start to know certain areas of the city fairly well. You might have a passing knowledge of Covent Garden, be familiar with a couple of the streets around Piccadilly or you could be able to find your way round little bits of the City. On the whole, though, you feel you only know "your" areas of London, and you've never joined them up.

Yet sometimes, if you forgo the Underground and take the bus, you suddenly realize how some of your

little pockets of local knowledge piece together: it dawns on you that, actually, you know more about the geography than you thought.

We hope that this friendly guide to what Elgar composed when may prove to work just like that for you. We have tried to join up the pockets of knowledge about what was "just around the corner" when Elgar was writing his great music. Sometimes historical and cultural events are known to have happened at the same time: the First World War and *The Music Makers*, for example. On other occasions, they may be eyebrow raising: *The Cockaigne Overture* and Picasso's "Blue Period". Now and again, they are downright surprising: Elgar and Rossini were composing at the same time.

Overall, though, the familiar nature of the events only serves to make the composer, who can sometimes seem almost institutional and other-worldly, feel much, much more real.

In the following chart, Elgar's age is set in relation to world events and his decades are also made clear. It is very easy for us always to imagine Elgar as an old man, because this is how he tends to be portrayed. However, by just taking a quick look at what was going on during his twenties and thirties, we see a far more human side to the man than is often remembered.

YEAR	Age	What was going on	What Elgar did
1857		Thomas Hughes' *Tom Brown's School Days* is published	Elgar born, 2 June, at Broadheath
1858	1	Offenbach premiered *Orpheus in the Underworld*	
1859	2	Dickens wrote *A Tale of Two Cities*. Wagner wrote *Tristan und Isolde*. Charles Darwin published *The Origin of Species*	Moved with family to Worcester
1860	3	Victor Emmanuel became king of Italy. Mahler born. George Eliot wrote *The Mill on the Floss*	
1861	4	Sandringham House built for Queen Victoria. Mrs Beeton published her *Book of Household Management*. *Tannhäuser* premiered	
1862	5	Verdi's *La Forza del Destino* premiered. Victor Hugo published *Les Misérables*	
1863	6	Abraham Lincoln gave the Gettysburg Address. Manet painted *Le petit Déjeuner sur l'Herbe*.	Started school
1864	7	Toulouse Lautrec born. Louis Pasteur invented pasteurization.	
1865	8	*Alice's Adventures in Wonderland* published. Abraham Lincoln assassinated	

CONTINUED ▶

YEAR	Age	What was going on	What Elgar did
1866	9	Alfred Nobel invented dynamite	
1867	10	Ibsen wrote *Peer Gynt*. Millais painted *Boyhood of Raleigh*	Wrote first piece, *Humoreske*
1868	11	Louisa M. Alcott wrote *Little Women*. Gladstone became British Prime Minister. Rossini died	
1869	12	Suez Canal opened. Gandhi born.	
1870	13	Lenin born. Tchaikovsky wrote *Romeo & Juliet Overture*	Heard Handel's *Messiah*. Started on violin
1871	14	Paris Commune. Proust born. Verdi wrote *Aida*	
1872	15	Diaghilev born. Jules Verne wrote *Around the World in Eighty Days*	Wrote musical (part of later *Wand of Youth*)
1873	16	Tolstoy wrote *Anna Karenina*. Rachmaninov born	Left school. Started work in solicitor's office
1874	17	Disraeli became British Prime Minister. Churchill born. Marconi born. Thomas Hardy wrote *Far from the Madding Crowd*	Left solicitor's to work in dad's music shop
1875	18	Mark Twain wrote *The Adventures of Tom Sawyer*. Bizet wrote *Carmen*. Ravel born	

1876	19	Wagner opened Bayreuth Opera House. Alexander Graham Bell invented the telephone	Played violin in orchestras. Wrote *Salve Regina* and *Tantum Ergo*
1877	20	Edison invented the phonograph. Queen Victoria became Empress of India. All-England Lawn Tennis Championship started at Wimbledon	Joined quintet, playing bassoon
1878	21	Gilbert & Sullivan wrote *HMS Pinafore*. London introduced electric street lighting	Made Music Director of Powick Lunatic Asylum Music Society
1879	22	Einstein born. British Zulu war. Tchaikovsky wrote *Eugene Onegin*	Moved to live with sister Pollie. Heard Saint-Saëns play organ in Paris
1880	23	Rodin sculpted *The Thinker*	
1881	24	Boer War in the Transvaal. Picasso born. Brahms wrote *Academic Festival Overture*	
1882	25	R. L. Stevenson wrote *Treasure Island*. Trollope died. Manet painted *Un Bar aux Folies Bergère*	Became violinist in Birmingham concert orchestra. Visited Leipzig, and heard Wagner and Schumann
1883	26	Paul Kruger became President of South Africa. Nietzsche wrote *Also Sprach Zarathustra*. Wagner died	Moved to live with other sister, Lucy. Became engaged to Helen Weaver
1884	27	Mark Twain wrote *The Adventures of Huckleberry Finn*. Massenet wrote *Manon*.	Engagement broken off. Played Dvořák's *Stabat Mater* at Three Choirs Festival, with Dvořák himself conducting. *Romance*, first published piece

CONTINUED

5

YEAR	Age	What was going on	What Elgar did
1885	28	Karl Benz builds car engine. Gordon of Khartoum killed. Zola wrote *Germinal*	Became organist at St George's Church, Worcester. Took on Alice Roberts as piano pupil
1886	29	R. L. Stevenson wrote *Dr Jekyll & Mr Hyde*. Rodin sculpted *The Kiss*	
1887	30	Queen Victoria celebrated her Golden Jubilee. Arthur Conan Doyle wrote *A Study in Scarlet* (first Sherlock Holmes story)	
1888	31	Kipling wrote *Plain Tales from the Hills*. Mahler became director of Budapest Opera. Dunlop invented pneumatic tyre. Jack the Ripper terrorized London	Became engaged to Alice. Wrote *Salut d'Amour* (orig. *Liebesgruss*) for her
1889	32	Cecil Rhodes granted Royal Charter for his British South Africa Co. Eiffel Tower erected for Paris Exhibition. Barnum and Bailey's circus came to London	Married Alice at London's Brompton Oratory. Sold *Salut d'Amour* for two guineas. Moved to London
1890	33	Oscar Wilde wrote *The Picture of Dorian Gray*. Van Gogh died. Cardinal Newman died. Mascagni wrote *Cavalleria Rusticana*	Wrote orchestral piece *Froissart*. Daughter, Carice, born
1891	34	Thomas Hardy wrote *Tess of the d'Urbevilles*. Rachmaninov wrote *Piano Concerto No. 1*	Moved to Malvern

1892	35	Keir Hardie became first Labour MP. Toulouse Lautrec painted *At the Moulin Rouge*	Wrote *Serenade for Strings*. Visited Bayreuth, and Beethoven's birthplace
1893	36	Cole Porter born. Tchaikovsky died. Dvořák wrote *Symphony No. 9 From the New World*.	
1894	37	Alfred Dreyfus deported to Devil's Island. Kipling wrote *The Jungle Book*. Sibelius wrote *Finlandia*	
1895	38	Tchaikovsky wrote *Swan Lake*. Gillette invented the safety razor. H. G. Wells wrote *The Time Machine*	
1896	39	Chekhov wrote *The Seagull* Puccini wrote *La Bohème*. Modern Olympics started in Athens	Wrote *King Olaf*
1897	40	Edmond Rostand wrote *Cyrano de Bergerac*. Brahms died. J. J. Thomson discovered the electron	Wrote *Chanson de Nuit*. Became conductor of the Worcestershire Philharmonic Society
1898	41	Zola published *"J'accuse"*. letter in Dreyfus affair. Gladstone died. Oscar Wilde wrote *The Ballad of Reading Gaol*	Wrote *Caractacus*, dedicated to Queen Victoria
1899	42	Boer War. Noel Coward born. Oscar Wilde wrote *The Importance of Being Earnest*	Wrote the *Enigma Variations*. Wrote *Chanson de Matin*. Wrote *Sea Pictures*
1900	43	Puccini wrote *Tosca*. Ramsay MacDonald became head of Labour Party. Sir Arthur Sullivan died	Wrote *The Dream of Gerontius*

CONTINUED ▶

7

YEAR	Age	What was going on	What Elgar did
1901	44	Queen Victoria died. Picasso began his Blue Period. Verdi died	Wrote *Cockaigne Overture* and *Pomp and Circumstance Marches Nos.1 and 2*
1902	45	Leon Trotsky settled in London. Debussy wrote *Pelléas & Mélisande*	Reworked *Pomp and Circumstance March No.1* into *Coronation Ode* (includes "*Land of Hope and Glory*")
1903	46	Wright Brothers invented the first manned aeroplane. Theodore Roosevelt became US President	
1904	47	Dvořák died. London Symphony Orchestra played first concert. Rolls-Royce Company founded	Elgar knighted. Moved to Hereford
1905	48	Einstein published *Relativity*. Léhar wrote *The Merry Widow*. Baroness Orczy wrote *The Scarlet Pimpernel*	Became Chair of Music at Birmingham University. Wrote *Introduction and Allegro for Strings*
1906	49	Cézanne died. Shostakovich born. Edward VII met Germany's William II	Elgar's father died
1907	50	Lumière Brothers invented colour photography. Picasso painted *Les Demoiselles d'Avignon*. Mahler wrote *Symphony of a Thousand (Symphony No. 8)*	Wrote *Pomp and Circumstance March No. 4*. Wrote *Symphony No. 1*
1908	51	Asquith became Prime Minister. Kenneth Grahame wrote *The Wind in the Willows*. Term Cubism coined	

1909	52	Henry Ford sold the first Model T. Vaughan Williams wrote *Fantasia on a Theme of Thomas Tallis*	Jaeger (*Nimrod*) died
1910	53	E. M. Forster wrote *Howard's End*. Murderer H. H. Crippen executed. George V succeeds Edward VII	Wrote *Violin Concerto*
1911	54	Revolution in China. Braque painted *Man with a Guitar*. Mahler died	Awarded the Order of Merit. Became conductor of the London Symphony Orchestra
1912	55	Stalin became editor of *Pravda*. Scott reached the South Pole. Delius wrote *On Hearing the First Cuckoo in Spring*	Moved to London (Hampstead). Wrote *The Music Makers*. Diagnosed with Ménière's Disease
1913	56	Arthur Wynne invented the crossword puzzle. *The Rite of Spring* incited riot in Paris. D. H. Lawrence wrote *Sons and Lovers*	Contract with LSO not renewed. Wrote *Falstaff*
1914	57	First World War. James Joyce wrote *Dubliners*. Panama Canal opened	Elgar recorded for HMV. Enrolled as a wartime Special Constable
1915	58	D. W. Griffith released *Birth of a Nation*. Somerset Maugham wrote *Of Human Bondage*	Joined the Hampstead Special Reserves. Wrote *The Starlight Express*
1916	59	Somme campaign began. Harold Brighouse wrote *Hobson's Choice*. Yehudi Menuhin born	

CONTINUED ▶

YEAR	Age	What was going on	What Elgar did
1917	60	Mata Hari executed. October Revolution in Russia. G. Grosz produced *The Face of the Ruling Classes* lithographs	Wrote *The Spirit of England*
1918	61	First World War ended. Rupert Brooke *Collected Poems* published posthumously. Parry died	Had his tonsils removed
1919	62	Mussolini founded Fascist Movement. Picasso designed sets for *The Three Cornered Hat*. Renoir died	Wrote the *Cello Concerto*
1920	63	League of Nations founded. Max Bruch died. Ravel wrote *La Valse*	Elgar's wife, Alice, died
1921	64	D. H. Lawrence wrote *Women in Love*. Charlie Chaplin starred in *The Kid*. Prokofiev wrote *The Love For Three Oranges*	Elgar's daughter, Carice, married
1922	65	USSR founded. James Joyce wrote *Ulysses*. Louis Armstrong joined King Oliver's Jazz band	
1923	66	P. G. Wodehouse wrote *The Inimitable Jeeves*. Douglas Fairbanks starred in *Robin Hood*. Gershwin wrote *Rhapsody in Blue*	Elgar made Master of the King's Music
1924	67	Fauré died. Stanley Baldwin became Prime Minister. First Winter Olympics held	

1925	68	John Logie Baird developed television. F. Scott Fitzgerald wrote *The Great Gatsby*. Kafka's *The Trial* published posthumously	Awarded the Royal Philharmonic Society Gold Medal
1926	69	General strike in Britain. A. A. Milne wrote *Winnie the Pooh*. Duke Ellington made his first record	
1927	70	German economy collapsed. Proust's *À La Recherche du Temps Perdu* published posthumously. Kern & Hammerstein premiered *Showboat*	
1928	71	Alexander Fleming discovered penicillin. Ravel wrote *Bolero*	
1929	72	Ernest Hemingway wrote *A Farewell to Arms*. St Valentine's Day Massacre in Chicago	Moved to Worcester
1930	73	Arthur Conan Doyle died. Marlene Dietrich starred in *The Blue Angel*. Hoagy Carmichael wrote *Georgia on my Mind*	Wrote the *Severn Suite*. Wrote *Pomp and Circumstance March No. 5*
1931	74	Dali painted *Persistence of Memory*. Empire State Building built	Wrote the *Nursery Suite*. Awarded a baronetcy. Elgar opened the new Abbey Road studios. Met Vera Hockman
1932	75	Edwin Land invented polaroid photography. De Valera became President of Ireland. Sir Thomas Beecham founded London Philharmonic Orchestra	Yehudi Menuhin recorded the *Violin Concerto*. Director General of BBC, Sir John Reith, commissioned *Third Symphony*

CONTINUED ▶

YEAR	Age	What was going on	What Elgar did
1933	76	Edwin Howard invented FM (frequency modulation) radio. Hitler became German Chancellor. George Orwell wrote *Down and Out in Paris and London*	Visited Delius in Grez-sur-Loing
1934		*Goodbye Mr Chips* published	Elgar died, 23 February

02

The Story of Elgar: The Cast List

Major roles

Elgar

Arguably, the greatest English composer who ever lived and, definitely, the owner of a handlebar moustache by which all others would forever be judged. What more needs to be said?

Alice

Elgar's wife, nine years his senior. Born Caroline Alice Roberts, the daughter of an English army officer. As we'll see, she became the driving force behind Elgar, pushing both him and his music, and acting, often, as his very first in-house critic.

Jaeger

Jaeger was an editor at Novello, Elgar's publisher. He consistently championed Elgar's music and was one of the first people to truly realize what England had on its hands in him. Sadly, as we'll see, both Jaeger and Alice predeceased Elgar (Jaeger by 25 years, Alice by 14 years). This meant that Elgar was without two vital promoters towards the end of his life.

"Windflower"

"Windflower" is Elgar's nickname for his friend Alice Stuart-Wortley (and as his wife was called Alice, too, it's the name we will use for her to avoid confusion). Elgar nicknamed her after the flowers growing wild in the Worcestershire countryside.

Pollie

One of Elgar's sisters, and possibly the one to whom he was closest. He lived with Pollie and her husband

when they first married and then again for a spell
when Alice died.

Minor roles

William Elgar

Elgar's father. Although billed here as an extra, it
was his music shop and piano tuning that would
provide the essential backdrop to and influence on
Elgar's early life.

Ann Elgar

Elgar's mother and possibly the person from whom
he inherited his love of the countryside.

Cameos

Look out for cameo appearances in our story from
the great violinist and conductor, Yehudi Menuhin;
and from the composer, and another great
conductor, Richard Strauss.

When Elgar Was Young

Before Elgar Was Born

"England has no music," said Ralph Waldo Emerson, just one year before Elgar was born, preempting the nickname "the land without music" by some 58 years. *"Das Land ohne Musik"* was an academic essay by Oscar Schmitz, written in 1914.

This sweeping statement was made chiefly about the state of England's composers. True, the country had concert halls, it had orchestras and it had visiting international stars, but it also had one major

musical problem: it was seen by everyone else to be lacking a renowned composer of its own. Soon, though, very soon, the melting pot of circumstances and talents would prove perfect for the right man with the right music. "Cometh the hour. . .," as they say.

England was an amazing place before Elgar was born. His father, William, and his mother, Ann, were born into a country currently being rejuvenated by its queen, Victoria. In 1856, already 19 years into her reign, 17 of those with her consort, Albert, she was overseeing the empire with style and panache. Charles Dickens was at his creative peak, with *Little Dorrit, Bleak House* and *David Copperfield* already published. *A Tale of Two Cities, Our Mutual Friend* and *Great Expectations* were still to come. International travel was being revolutionized by the Cunard Line, which was fairly whisking folk across the Atlantic on its ocean-going liners in a giddying 9½ days.

Other world events included the discovery, in 1855, by Livingstone of the Victoria Falls, a jaw-dropping waterfall on the Zambezi River, which he had "claimed" for his queen. And Big Ben was born when, in 1858, Sir Benjamin Halls, the Director of Public Works, oversaw the casting of a 13½ ton bell in the Whitechapel Bell Foundry, designed to sit in St Stephen's Tower of the Houses of Parliament.

In your *Daily Telegraph* – the new paper which had commenced publication in 1855 – you might have read about Florence Nightingale, the remarkable English nurse who was pioneering new standards of hygiene in the military field-hospitals of the Crimea; about the newly opened National Portrait Gallery and the Museum of Ornamental Art (later, in 1899, refashioned as the Victoria and Albert Museum); about the newly formed Alpine Club of London; or about Charles Hallé's "Hallé Concerts" in Manchester.

Perhaps more pertinent for Elgar's father and his immediate prospects, within just a few years of each other, the Bechstein and the Steinway dynasties had begun. Karl Bechstein set up his piano factory in 1856 in Berlin, while Heinrich E. Steinweg changed his name to Henry Steinway and, with his three sons, set up the company that was to become the most famous name in pianos, in New York, in 1853. Parlour room music was the soap opera of its day, and pianos were the televisions.

Elgar's Birth

William Elgar was a piano tuner, music shop manager, organist and violinist. He tuned pianos in the well-to-do houses of Worcestershire and he ran a shop in "The Cross" in the centre of Worcester. He also played the organ at the Catholic church of St George, just a minute's walk round the corner, a

job he had acquired in 1856; and he played the
violin in local orchestras and at his "Glee Club" –
an informal gathering of musicians that met every
week in a local hotel.

William had married his wife, Ann, in 1848, and
they soon had a young son, Harry. Four years later,
she gave birth to Lucy Ann. Pollie followed in
1854. Some three years afterwards, they moved the
family three or so miles out of the centre of
Worcester to Broadheath. Home was now The Firs,
a simple double-fronted cottage, with shutters on
the downstairs windows and a roof double-ended by
two quaint chimney pots. It was here that Elgar was
born, on 2 June, 1857.

Nine days later, his dad took him to "work", as it
were, to St George's Church in Worcester, where he
was christened Edward William Elgar.

Elgar was the fourth of what would eventually be
seven children. The order runs: Harry (Henry
John), Lucy Ann, Pollie (Susannah Mary), Edward,
Jo (Frederick Joseph), Frank (Francis Thomas) and
Dot (Helen Agnes). Sadly, not all seven would
survive into adulthood, a tragic yet common-
enough story in Victorian England.

When Elgar was born, his father would spend the
weekdays in Worcester – tending his music store –
and the weekends in Broadheath, where musical

evenings around the piano were a common
occurrence on Saturday nights.

When Elgar Was Two . . .

When Elgar was two, his father moved the
entire family to 1 Edgar Street in Worcester,
much to his mother's annoyance. She had been
much happier in the countryside of Broadheath
so, for her, the relative bustle of life in central
Worcester was far from ideal. Now called Severn
Street, 1 Edgar Street was just a few minutes'
walk from William's job at St George's church.
The family lived above the music shop. But not
for long.

When Elgar Was Three . . .

When Elgar was three, the family moved again,
both home and shop. By now, business-wise,
things appeared to be looking up for William.
He had scouted new shop premises at 10 High
Street in Worcester. Again, they lived above the
shop and business appeared to be good – so good,
in fact, that William invited his brother, Elgar's
Uncle Henry, to join him to help run the place.
They had worked together previously, but had
parted company after an argument. Now, a fresh
sign was painted which proudly proclaimed
"Elgar Brothers".

When Elgar Was Four . . .

When Elgar was four, the family, including Uncle Henry, moved again, this time to 2 College Precincts, the house in which William and Ann had lived when they were first married. While they were there, on 1 October, 1861, Elgar's brother, Frank (Thomas Francis) was born. The little babe would have known little of College Precincts, though, because within a couple of years they were on the move yet again.

When Elgar Was Six . . .

The family moved back to the rooms above the shop at 10 High Street. It may be that all this shuttling back and forwards from place to place made some kind of impression on Elgar, who, in later life, would be forever upping sticks and moving on from house to house (not to mention a myriad different summer homes).

It was around now that Elgar started school. His sisters, Lucy and Pollie, had been attending a school at 11 Britannia Square, run by a Miss Caroline Walsh and, in the September of 1863, Elgar joined them. Although it is often rightly said that Elgar became very attached to his mother from this early age, it was, in fact, his father who noticed Elgar's talent for music. Soon enough, William arranged music lessons for his

21

son, first of all with one of the singers from his choir at St George's – Sarah Rickets – and then with one of the teachers at 11 Britannia Square – Pollie Tyler.

At this point, Elgar learned to play the piano and it was said that he was able to ad lib amazingly on the instrument. His father would even take him to neighbours' houses to have them hear his son's great talent for "extemporization".

It was also around this time that Elgar would have first started travelling with his father on his piano-tuning round. By now, William was tuning pianos in some of the most well-to-do homes in the area. He had taken to doing his rounds by pony and trap, with the young Edward beside him, trotting through the leafy, Worcestershire countryside from job to job. It's easy to understand how Elgar's music took on this wonderfully positive association with nature and idyllic journeys by horse and cart – a beautiful influence on the young Elgar which can't be underestimated (although two other associations would also be added to the mix to make create the heady Elgarian signature sound: more on this in a moment).

In later life, on journeys through Worcestershire, Elgar would often regale friends with stories of who used to live in which house, which people had which pianos; and he would even provide a commentary on the stable folk who had tended his father's horses when they stopped off. Sadly, for Elgar, this gentle, halcyon life was about to be shattered.

When Elgar Was Seven . . .

When Elgar was seven, tragedy hit his family. His 15-year-old brother, Harry, became ill with a kidney disease. Within a matter of just a few weeks, the disease claimed his life. Despite the common nature of childhood mortality at this time, the bereavement nevertheless hit the entire family hard, not least Elgar, who now became the eldest son.

When Elgar Was Nine . . .

When Elgar was nine, tragedy struck once again. This time, it was Elgar's younger brother, Jo, who contracted TB in the summer of 1866. By September that year, he was dead and the family was once again grief-stricken. This early encounter with the spectre of death and family bereavement may mean that, into the mix of music and nature, was thrown melancholy – a trio of influences that would often prove a potent blend.

Jo died on 7 September, 1863. It so happened that the Three Choirs Festival – an event shared between Worcester, Hereford and Gloucester, happening, then, every three years at one of the town's cathedrals – was that year scheduled for Worcester. Elgar's father was down to play violin in the orchestra for Beethoven's *Mass in C minor* (his Uncle Henry was playing viola). So, in order to deflect his attention from Jo's death, Elgar was taken along to all the rehearsals of this amazing work. He was utterly moved by the music. He is said to have remarked that he would have loved to have had the orchestra do *his* bidding, then who knows what they could have achieved.

The Three Choirs Festival

The Three Choirs Festival is one of the oldest surviving music festivals in the UK, with a history traceable back to the 18th century. It's a "three-centre" festival, taking place every year in one of Gloucester, Hereford or Worcester, and is largely centred on the cathedrals. Once he became involved, Elgar never looked back: he and his music were associated with the Three Choirs Festival right up until he died. The festival has occasionally stopped – for reasons such as war – but, apart from that, it is still going strong, with The Philharmonia, Classic FM's Orchestra on Tour, now resident at the festival each year.

One of the priests from St George's gave him a small engraving of St Joseph, which bore a small inscription: "Jesus, Mary and Joseph – pray for me in my own agony." The words were, in fact, a quotation from *The Dream of Gerontius* by the then Father Newman (later Cardinal).

This made up the fourth of the early influences which would stay with Elgar all his life – music, nature, melancholy and religion.

When Elgar Was 10 . . .

When Elgar was 10, something pretty important happened. Now living in Worcester, the family decided to take a summer holiday back in Broadheath Common. Maybe Elgar's mother, Ann, was missing it? Whatever the reason, it meant that Elgar found himself on a farm, in Broadheath Common, not far from the family's old house. It was here that he wrote his very first piece of music. It was called *Humoreske* and he was later to describe it as a bit of a jape. In a way, it was a bit of a "musical joke" – a game, if you like, and a fitting first outing for the man who was going to become famous with musical game-playing in the *Enigma Variations*.

When Elgar Was 11 . . .

Elgar moved schools from Miss Walsh's to Spetchley Park, where the Berkeley family ran a private Catholic school on their estate, nearly three miles on the way out of Worcester, towards Stratford.

When Elgar Was 12 . . .

Elgar eventually changed schools in favour of
Littleton House, in Wick, a small establishment
with only 30-odd pupils, which was run by another
Catholic teacher called Reeve. Here, he made his
first real friend, fellow pupil Hubert Leicester.
Although Leicester was two years older than Elgar,
the two were thrown together because they used to
share the journey to school. Leicester would go on
to describe Elgar as both shy and mature and yet
also very fond of a bit of tomfoolery. Also,
according to Leicester, Elgar spent a large amount
of time off school, through either illness or truancy.

It was around this time, too, that Elgar, together
with his brothers and sisters, put together a family
play for their parents. It was on the theme of a
woodland glade which was barred to the adult
world. While all the children took part in the play,
it was Elgar who wrote and arranged the tunes – the
incidental music, if you like – for the youthful
offering. They may have been the tunes of a 12-
year-old boy but, a long way off in the future, they
would be put to very good use indeed.

Elgar had an early meeting with the music of
Handel, too, when he was 12. He had managed to
hear the *Messiah* aria, *"O Thou That Tellest"* at a
public performance and, within weeks, had taught
himself to play it. He also took part in writing out

the orchestral part to the *Messiah*, taking the liberty of adding some extra notes of his own, for "colourful" good measure – notes that were spotted at the rehearsals. This Handel run-in somehow had the effect of making Elgar aware that he wanted to take up the violin, professionally, and, from that day, he began to teach himself to play.

When Elgar Was 15 . . .

Elgar left Littleton House school, where he was Head Boy, and decided to try his luck on the employment market. With the help of his father's connections, he was taken on at William Allen's, a firm of solicitors. Elgar was to be taught the principles of the legal profession and the young man immediately buckled down to a year of hard work. It was a year that also saw him standing in for his father at St George's, and even doing his first violin gig. The venue, the Union Workhouse, on Tallow Hill, has long since been demolished and is now the site of flats called Byfield Rise.

When Elgar Was 16 . . .

When he was 16, Elgar felt he was simply not making enough progress at Allen's. Yes, he had learnt the basics of legal book-keeping, but much of his time had been occupied with more menial tasks, such as making tea and washing the floors. So, he decided to leave, and persuaded his father to take him on as an assistant in the family music shop. In fact, by all accounts, his book-keeping skills might have come in handy for his father, William, who was perhaps not the best man when it came to having a head for figures and business.

The music shop was a very important place for Elgar, because, for the first time, he was exposed to music all day, six days a week. He surrounded himself with music scores, often going off into the fields, with a ploughman's lunch, to simply sit and take them in.

This was the time during which he probably developed his amazing ability to "hear" music. As obvious as this may sound, not all musicians can truly hear music in the way some great composers can.

To draw a banal analogy, imagine you are redesigning a room. Some people have the ability to look at a room and instantly "see" the new one: how it will look, where you will walk, the colours, the textures, even though the room is still a wreck. Well, great musicians – and definitely Elgar – often have a similar power, but in their ears. They can look at a score, often a full score for orchestra, and their "inner ears" allow them to "hear" it. Everyone has the potential to do this, to some extent or other, it's just that great musicians are lucky enough to have developed it.

Elgar would, then, take scores to bed at night, much as a teenager today might read a Harry Potter under the bedclothes and be lost in a world of wizards and fantasy; but he was escaping to another magical, musical world.

One of the earliest scores he became truly engrossed with was Beethoven's *Pastoral Symphony*. He had an early fondness, in fact, for many of Beethoven's symphonies. When he was 16, he arranged a setting of the *"Credo"* for St George's, made up entirely of tunes from Beethoven symphonies.

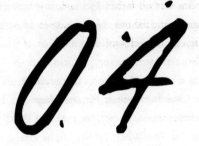

The Jobbing Musician

When Elgar Was 18 . . .

Musically speaking, two of the big events of 1875 were the premiere of Bizet's opera *Carmen* in Paris, and that composer's untimely death on 3 June. Just one day earlier, Elgar turned 18. Did he celebrate with a pint in his father's favourite pub, the Hop Market Hotel, in Sansome Street?

By November that year, Elgar was playing in the string section of the Worcester Music Society performance of Spohr's oratorio, *The Last Judgement*. Alongside him in the desks of second violins was his father, William. Soon afterwards, Elgar branched out into a separate orchestra when he landed a job as a member of a touring opera company, giving performances of operas such as Verdi's *Il Trovatore* and *La Traviata* as well as Mozart's *Don Giovanni*.

He also began taking violin lessons with one Fred Spray, the leader of the Glee Club Orchestra, although these ended some six months later, with Spray telling Elgar that there was nothing else he could teach him – a sign of his increasingly virtuosic violin technique.

When Elgar Was 19 . . .

True enough, by the time Elgar played in a performance of Mendelssohn's *Elijah*, the following year, he had been promoted to a first violinist. Perhaps uncomfortably for Elgar, his father was still back playing with the second violins. Elgar was now regularly deputizing for his father at St George's, too, something which was said to have led to the odd family argument. As autumn approached that year, Elgar was sufficiently inspired by his work at St George's to produce his first compositions for the choir – a setting of the *"Salve Regina"* and the *"Tantum Ergo"*.

Elgar started putting his violin technique to further good use, beyond simply concert performances, by taking on local pupils. Teaching was something at which Elgar candidly admitted he did not excel, but it brought him valuable income in these early days before fame and fortune beckoned.

When Elgar Was 20 . . .

The violin was rapidly becoming the major weapon in Elgar's armoury when it came to earning a living. His compositions, at this stage, numbered a mere handful. This year, he added *Reminiscences*, a violin and piano piece, to a youthful list, complete with its dedication to the local grocer. It now occurred to Elgar that he might one day make his way in the world as a concert violinist. He heard a performance by August Wilhelmj which further enthused him. Wilhelmj was the Konzertmeister at the Bayreuth Festival, as well as being one of the greatest violinists of his day, briefly hailed as "the next Paganini". His performances at the Royal Albert Hall in 1877 inspired the 20-year-old Elgar to save up his hard-earned money in order to buy himself some lessons with a truly great teacher in London.

Elgar chose Adolphe Pollitzer as his teacher. Pollitzer had played with various opera and symphony orchestras in London, before becoming Professor of Violin at the London Academy of Music in 1861. In the end, Elgar managed to have only five lessons with Pollitzer before his money ran out, but he was greatly encouraged by his new teacher. Pollitzer would come to play another crucial role in Elgar's development, as we will see a little later in our *Friendly Guide*.

Back home, Elgar's musical life continued to thrive. He became the leader of a brand new "rehearsal orchestra", the Amateur Instrumental Society (AIS) of Worcester. Elgar also managed to form his own wind quintet, made up of some of the members of the AIS. The quintet comprised Elgar's brother, Frank, on oboe, his friends, Hubert Leicester and Frank Exton, on flutes and Hubert's brother, William, on clarinet. Elgar himself played bassoon, an instrument on which he was totally self-taught. The quintet met regularly in a shed behind the Elgar family shop every Sunday and Elgar himself began to compose and arrange for them – his "shed music" as he called it.

The music written for the shed quintet ranges from full-scale chamber works lasting nearly half an hour, to youthful, jokey pieces written to a challenging weekly deadline. A quick look at the titles reveals a 20-year-old's tongue firmly in its cheek: *Somniferous*, *Hell and Tommy*, and the *Evesham Andante*; not to mention the intriguing *Mrs Winslow's Soothing Syrup* – a work of less than four minutes, named after a medicine of the day. Nevertheless, despite the humorous and musically immature nature of the "shed music", the discipline of writing what was to become almost two years'-worth of works, each week, for a mixed quintet would prove invaluable to Elgar, the composer.

When Elgar Was 21 . . .

More lessons with Pollitzer followed in 1878. By now, though, as well as his ever-growing skill on the violin, he was beginning to show his talent as a composer. He showed a number of his compositions to Pollitzer, who, in turn, introduced him to the then legendary figure of August Manns.

Manns was at that time the conductor of a series of influential concerts at the famous Crystal Palace. He was an amazing figure in music in 1878, having been responsible for all the music for the daily concerts held at the London venue for some 40 years. It was he who introduced much of the significant romantic music to the London audience. Manns gave Elgar a rehearsal pass, allowing him to attend the UK premieres of many new romantic works, although the privilege didn't come without its sacrifice.

In order to attend the rehearsals, Elgar left his house at 6 am, arriving at the concert hall by around 12 noon. Having sometimes heard only an hour or so of the rehearsal and then the concert, he would then leave again at 5 pm, arriving home as late as 11.30 or 12 pm – a day involving up to 12 hours of travelling to hear often only one hour of the rehearsal. Nevertheless, to Elgar, it was worth it.

When the Three Choirs Festival came around in the autumn of 1878 – it was Worcester's turn this year – Elgar was in the second violin section of the orchestra, playing works such as Mozart's *Symphony No. 40*. The piece must have left quite an impression on the young composer because he soon decided to use it as a model for a composition exercise of his own. He set himself the challenge of writing a work with exactly the same number of bars and with the same musical shape as Mozart's great symphony.

Elgar was every inch the image of the hopeful, jobbing musician – playing in local concerts, filling in for his father on the church organ and writing music whenever possible. He was always on the lookout for a secure musical post, though and, this year, 1878, it came – from an interesting source.

The Worcester County Pauper and Lunatic Asylum was built in 1847 on a site of more than 46 acres between Malvern and Worcester. Eventually, it would become the Powick Hospital, before being almost completely demolished to make way for housing. Only part of the main building still survives today and it has been converted into flats.

Back then, as well as 200 inmates, there was a large team of physicians, assistants and attendants, many of them musical. In 1878, the post of bandmaster was advertised, to run the ensemble of staff which gathered regularly to perform. Elgar applied by sending in one of his compositions and promptly got the job. As intriguing as the job sounds – Bandmaster at the County Lunatic Asylum – it would provide Elgar with yet another invaluable "practice orchestra". For the next five years, he could write music, conduct it, and get to know the nuances of its orchestration – priceless experience for any budding composer.

Elgar started his new job just hours after the firstfooters had seen in the New Year of 1879, on a salary of £32 per year, with an extra five shillings for every new composition he supplied. It may have been this renewed financial impetus to compose, or simply the demands of his busier lifestyle, which led Elgar to start to keep a composition notebook at around this time. In it, he would jot down any ideas for works and tunes, no matter how brief, with a view to using them later.

When Elgar Was 22 . . .

1879 was also an important year in another way: Elgar left home. His sister, Pollie, had recently married, becoming Pollie Grafton and, as was often the custom at the time, Elgar went to live with her

and her husband just around the corner, at 35
Chestnut Walk.

When Elgar Was 23. . .

As the autumn of 1880 drew in, Elgar made a visit
to Paris with the man who would become his
brother-in-law, Charles Pipe. He was courting
Elgar's other sister, Lucy. While in Paris, Elgar was
able to visit the city's second most famous church,
La Madeleine, where he heard the composer Saint-
Saëns playing the organ. By that time, another
famous French composer, Fauré, was the resident
organist. (Saint-Saëns had handed over the position
four years earlier.) In addition to the regular tourist
activities, such as taking in a Molière play, Elgar
absorbed many of the sights and sounds of the
French capital, writing a piece, *Paris*, on his return.

In the spring of 1881, his musical output continued
apace, with a march, the *Pas Redoublé*, and *Air de
Ballet*, both receiving performances from the
Amateur Instrumental Society in Worcester.

When Elgar Was 24 . . .

By the time the Three Choirs Festival came around
in late 1881, Elgar was playing in a performance of
Alexander Mackenzie's cantata *The Bride*. In
October, he was able to head into London to take
in concerts conducted by Hans Richter.

As we will see later in our *Friendly Guide,* Richter is an important name in the Elgar story. He was one of the foremost conductors of his day and on very friendly terms with Wagner, whose music he did much to promote. Although, by 1881, he was the Principal Conductor of the Vienna Philharmonic Orchestra, he had also established a series of concerts each year in London, known as the "Richter Concerts". To the British music-loving public, he was one of the biggest names in the orchestral world, a little piece of the great Teutonic tradition on their doorstep. This year, Elgar was in the audience to hear him play works by Berlioz and Wagner. The 24-year-old composer was extremely impressed.

More Elgar performances followed in 1882, if only on a very small scale. His *Air de Ballet* was repeated not once, but twice. At one performance, for a conference of the BMA, Elgar was greeted afterwards by one of the delegates, a Dr Charles Buck. He ran a GP practice in the Yorkshire Dales town of Settle and was an enthusiastic amateur cellist in his spare time. In fact, Buck had been playing in Elgar's orchestra at the BMA conference in order to bump up the numbers.

When Elgar Was 25 . . .

The composer and the doctor obviously hit it off and, before the summer was out, Elgar was visiting

Buck in his Ribblesdale home. He would become a regular guest at Buck's, taking long walks with the doctor, occasionally being invited to tennis parties at the homes of Buck's friends. A plaque in Market Place, Settle, commemorates Elgar's friendship with Buck, on the building that was then his surgery, but is now a NatWest bank.

Back in Worcester, Elgar wrote a small piano piece called *Douce Pensée* and managed to find enough spare time to get in some tennis and golf. The latter was to become one of Elgar's major pastimes.

A Round of Golf

Elgar was a keen golfer. One of the people immortalized in the Enigma Variations, *Richard Townshend, is credited with getting him interested. Elgar would often be seen sporting golfing plus-fours or a golf blazer and was also a member of Worcestershire Golf Club. You can see his clubs if you visit the Elgar Birthplace Museum. The composer himself considered it* "the best form of exercise for writing men, as it involves no risk of accident".

Professionally, Elgar would still have been known at this time as a violinist. He had now progressed from being the leader of the Amateur Instrumental Society to its conductor and had also gained a place in a concert orchestra, which meant regular journeys to perform in Birmingham.

See You in Birmingham!

While the music festival circuit of today, which takes in cities such as Edinburgh, Bath, Brighton and Canterbury, for example, is thriving, it is nothing compared to the amazing festival circuit that existed in Elgar's day. Back then, before the real advent of cinema, let alone television, most towns and cities had music festivals: Leeds, Birmingham, Hereford, Worcester, Llandrindod Wells – you name it, the town probably had a festival. As a result, there was a constant rotating circuit, much like the social circuit that today surrounds Ascot, Wimbledon and Cowes, which constantly needed feeding with new works. As each festival had its own chorus, many of the works needed for performance were oratorios or cantatas. This circuit was as important for orchestras as it was for choirs, and as important for conductors as it was for composers. It attested to the amazing, musical health of the nation in Victorian and Edwardian Britain.

It was around this time that one of Elgar's first loves developed. In October 1882, he finished a polka entitled *La Blonde*, which he dedicated to an H.J.W. These were the initials of Helen Weaver. Elgar may possibly have known Helen from his early years back in his father's shop. Helen's father owned the shoe shop on Worcester High Street, just a few doors down from Elgar's father's music shop. They would almost certainly have met via Frank Weaver, Helen's brother, with whom Elgar played much of his amateur music. By 1882, Helen was studying music in Leipzig, something Elgar would have sorely loved to have done. Perhaps smitten, he managed to save up enough money from his music-making to afford a trip to Leipzig to see her, booking himself into the same pension as the object of his affections. He arrived in Leipzig on 31 December and, so the story goes, he was immediately mistaken for a New Year's Eve reveller by the pension owner. Much to the amusement of his party, he was shepherded into a roomful of carousing Germans, all of them with tankards aloft. Elgar, not the best German speaker in the world, is said to have merely politely bowed and left pretty quickly.

Despite the real reason for his visit, Elgar nevertheless took the time to enjoy lots of world-class music in Leipzig. He took in performances of Wagner's operas *Tannhäuser*, *Lohengrin* and *Parsifal*, and was particularly struck by the famous Leipzig Gewandhaus Orchestra, which he managed to hear rehearsing Schumann. The orchestra was conducted by Carl Reinecke at the time and Elgar was impressed that they started their rehearsals at 9 o'clock in the morning. In addition to the professional concerts, though, there were musical soirées in the pension, which gave him the chance to be with Helen. And here comes the big question – did Elgar propose to Helen Weaver? He certainly once referred to her as "Braut" in his letters – the German word for bride – but this could just as easily been Elgar being jokey.

Back in England, Elgar heard more of the music of
the recently deceased Wagner at a Crystal Palace
concert. He also moved house, from one sister's
home to another's. Pollie and her husband were
relocating to Stoke Prior, near Bromsgrove, and so
from the spring of 1883, Elgar went to live with his
other sister, Lucy Pipe, at her house at 4 Field
Terrace, Worcester. As we will see, Elgar's penchant
for moving from house to house almost bordered
on the nomadic.

A new work was finished not long afterwards, the
Intermezzo: Serenade Mauresque, which was accepted
for performance by the Worcester Musical Union
and repeated later in the year. All the time, Elgar
was effectively "practising" his composition – taking
in as much music as he could by night, and writing
as much as he could, when time allowed, by day.
This side of Elgar is important to remember and it
is a theme that comes back again and again in his
music: Elgar was a practical musician. As he would
pointedly say, later on in life when speaking at
Birmingham University, he came up through the
ranks of real musicians, rather than being an
academic. He attended no music college.
His compositional style was formed through lots
of self-teaching and reading and by taking in as
much music as he could. What came out, though,
was distinctive Elgar – it was his own style,
forged through musicianship, not
musicology.

He heard a performance of the Berlioz *Requiem*, again at the Crystal Palace, no doubt somewhat distracted by thoughts of the imminent return of Helen Weaver to England.

When Elgar Was 26 . . .

He deferred a trip to visit Charles Buck in Settle to be around when Helen arrived. Elgar finished a new work, the polka *Helcia*, before eventually catching up with Buck for a brief holiday. Sadly, Helen's mother was dying and Helen's return to England was totally taken up with her care and her subsequent death in November. Helen did, however, find time to hear some of Elgar's music played in a concert in Birmingham. It was the *Intermezzo* he had written earlier in the year and both she and Elgar's mother were there to hear the premiere. It appears to have gone down well with both the audience and the critics – one describing it as "*a musicianly work*" and pointing out that Elgar certainly had potential.

The year 1884 opened with Elgar outlining his money troubles to a friend in a letter. He wrote:

I have no money – not a cent.

Interestingly, Helen was by now referred to as "Miss Weaver", rather than anything more familiar. Thankfully, his musical world was looking up. His new orchestral piece, *Sevillana*, was premiered on 1

May in Worcester and, better still, with his teacher
Adolphe Pollitzer having put a word in for him, it
was repeated at a Crystal Palace concert not long
afterwards. This was a milestone for Elgar – the first
time his music had ever been heard in London.
Helen Weaver may have broken off their
"engagement" – indeed, it is possible she was ill,
too – but, musically, everything was going in the
right direction. Well, almost everything.

When Elgar Was 27 . . .

Inspired once again by a performance of Beethoven's
Violin Concerto, Elgar ventured to ask Pollitzer if he
would ever make it as a concert violinist. The
answer came back: "No!" Although Elgar must have
been devastated, he also might have been slightly
relieved. Pollitzer had, in some respects, done him
and the world a favour in grabbing Elgar firmly by
the shoulders, turning him around, and pointing
him, once and for all, away from the door marked
"performer" and towards the one marked
"composer". From this point on, the violin became
simply work: composition became the career.

A brief holiday to Scotland, taking in Mull and
Iona, produced a small piece for violin and piano,
Une Idylle, with its enigmatic dedication to "E.E"
from Inverness. If Elgar were on the rebound, then
it was only briefly, as nothing else was heard of E.E.
ever again. Of course, it's always possible that E.E.

is some odd reference to himself, but unlikely. September's Three Choirs Festival was enough to put all other thoughts out of his head, anyway. This year, 1884, Worcester had pulled off a coup – the 43-year-old Bohemian composer, Dvořák, was coming to town. Elgar played in both his *Stabat Mater* and his *Symphony No. 6.*

He must have been in heaven – within spitting distance of one of the world's greatest composers, marvelling at, indeed being a part of, Dvořák's mighty and colourful orchestration. This inspiration, combined with Pollitzer's comments from earlier in the year, was enough to make Elgar realize he must concentrate on his composition. Within a month, he had resigned from his job as Bandmaster at the Powick County Lunatic Asylum.

Early signs were good. By November, he had had his Opus 1 published. This was his first catalogued work. It was the *Romance in E Minor for Violin and Piano* and it was bought by the publisher Schott for just one shilling – plus 20 free copies to keep for himself. He received no royalties but, at least, he was off the mark.

When Elgar Was 28 . . .

It would seem that 1885 was a mixed-up year. Elgar spent a number of holidays with Charles Buck up in Settle. Again, there was talk of romance, this time with a Sarah-Anne Wilkinson, daughter of a well-to-do merchant from the nearby town of Hellifield. Surviving pictures from the time show the moustachioed Elgar standing, with one hand resting on Sarah-Anne's chair. By all accounts, her father put the kibosh on Elgar's chances. The penniless son of a tradesman marrying his daughter? Not a chance. As if to put the seal on an end to romance, Elgar received news that Helen Weaver was emigrating to New Zealand.

These were interesting times at St George's, in Worcester, too. His father had parted company with the church some years earlier, after a disagreement over the way things were being run. Elgar must have had mixed feelings when asked to take over from his father's successor in the October of this year. William Elgar had put in 37 years' service in the organ loft. His son now began a smaller but perhaps more significant four-year reign.

In February 1886, Elgar was back in the orchestra at Birmingham, this time to play in the massive Verdi *Requiem*, a work that was then only 12 years old. It had received its British premiere in 1875 at the Albert Hall, with Verdi himself conducting, but this was the first time Birmingham had had the chance to stage the mighty choral piece.

As spring arrived, Elgar went to hear the British premiere of Bruckner's two-year-old *Symphony No. 7*, and managed to get to the Crystal Palace, too, where he witnessed Liszt, on his final visit to England.

Regal Dan Sword (or Elgar and Words)

As the anagrammatic title of this mini-section suggests, Elgar had a thing about words. His friends from school attested to this fact early on and it was something he never lost. It manifested itself often in wordplays, as in the title of his house "Craeg Lea" (which is an anagram of the letters E, A & C Elgar – that is, Edward, Alice and Carice Elgar). Even Elgar's daughter's name, which he first applied to his wife, is a conjoining of the words CARoline and alICE. An early telegraphic address of Elgar's was "Siromoris", a deliberately palindromic word.

This love of puzzles and wordplay would eventually show itself in his music, not just in the initials intriguingly applied to each movement of the Enigma Variations, *but also in places such as the dedication of his* Violin Concerto, *where he left five blanks after the line* "Here is enshrined the soul of . . . . ." *to tease future generations.*

When Elgar Was 29 ...

Without the Powick job as a steady means of getting the money in, Elgar decided to take on more pupils. His father's music shop had been well known in the area for more than 30 years by this time, so he didn't want for new students, despite his reputation for being not the most temperate of teachers. So it was that Elgar's advert for his piano lessons caught the eye of one Caroline Alice Roberts. Alice, as she preferred to be called, was the daughter of a retired colonel who had served in the British army in India before retiring to Redmarley d'Abitot, a small village near Ledbury, in Gloucestershire. Alice was herself born in Bombay. As well as studying piano, she was an enthusiastic writer of both poetry and novels. She began piano lessons with Elgar in October.

By March the following year, the relationship between Alice and Elgar had gone beyond that of teacher and pupil. Elgar was clearly taken with Alice enough to dedicate his latest song, *"Through the Long Days"* to "Miss Roberts", with words by the former statesman (and one-time secretary to Abraham Lincoln) turned poet, John Hay. Oddly, the words appear to be more a paean to Helen Weaver than anything directed at Alice:

Through the long days and years
  What will my loved one be,
    Parted from me?
Through the long days and years . . .

. . . Never on earth again
  Shall I before her stand,
    Touch her lip or hand,
Never on earth again.

But while my darling lives,
*   Peaceful, I journey on . . ."*

Alice's father had already died, so when her mother
passed away in 1887, Alice was totally alone. Elgar
lent her his copy of a poem by Cardinal John
Henry Newman, *The Dream of Gerontius*, complete
with its notes copied word for word from the
markings found in General Gordon's copy of the
work, discovered after his death at Khartoum.

The Dream of Gerontius

John Henry Newman was a Church of England minister
whose conversion to Catholicism in the 1840s caused a bit
of a stir. He wrote and gave talks on the subject of religion
and was responsible for many religious poems, the most
notable being The Dream of Gerontius. *When the British*
army officer, General Gordon, was killed at Khartoum, he
was found to have a copy of The Dream of Gerontius *on*
him. He had annotated it with his own comments. This
annotated version gained almost cult status – people would
copy out Gordon's comments into their own book and the
poem was eventually made available commercially, complete
with Gordon's notes. Elgar himself had a copy of the
"Gordon" version of Gerontius *– it was one of his favourite*
texts – and it was inevitable that he would one day set it to
his own music.

Alice eventually moved from Redmarley d'Abitot to a house called Saetermo (presumably after the Norwegian coastal town) in Great Malvern. At this time, Elgar was just 29 and Alice was 38.

When Elgar Was 30 . . .

Elgar continued to try to get his name known and his pieces played. Playing in the Three Choirs orchestra no doubt helped. 1887 saw premieres of works by Sullivan and Stanford. Elgar's *Three Pieces for Strings* were performed in Worcester and, although they are now lost, they would eventually be reworked by Elgar to form what we now know as his *Serenade for Strings*.

From this year onwards, he also began to set Alice's poems, such as *"The Wind at Dawn"*, to music. This particular work was published in *The Magazine of Music*.

When Elgar Was 31 . . .

August saw another important early composition, written on one of his many trips to Settle. It bears an inscription that features one of the earliest known examples of Elgar's fondness for wordplay, dedicated, as it was, "à Carice". Carice was a combining of Caroline Alice and would eventually become the name he gave to his only daughter. He called the piece *Liebesgruss*, which is German for "Love's Greeting".

The dedication obviously did the trick as, in September, he announced that their two-and-a-half year courtship was at an end. He was now engaged to Caroline Alice Roberts. Although Alice's parents themselves were not around to raise their eyebrows – the daughter of a respected Army colonel marrying a lowly, itinerant musician! – some of the members of her family did their best to live up to the stereotype. One aunt promptly cut Alice out of her will. Elgar was also a Roman Catholic, very much the wrong side of the religious tracks as far as the Establishment was concerned. At this time, Catholics had only been allowed for the last 60 years to hold public office. As if living up to the picture painted of him, it was a few months before Elgar could actually afford an engagement ring, made of pearl, to give to his fiancée. It has also been pointed out that, with her age – now 40 to his 31 – there were some who considered Alice an indecorously late entrant into the marrying game.

Despite all that they may have had against them, they set the big day for 8 May, 1889. At a sparse ceremony at London's Brompton Oratory, they were married. Elgar's sister Pollie and her husband, plus Elgar's Uncle Henry, swelled the meagre ranks on his side, while Alice's cousin and his wife were the only guests sitting on the bride's side.

In a bold step, Elgar decided that they should relocate to London – if he was going to make it as a composer, he had to move to London. The newly weds moved into 3 Marloes Road, in West Kensington. If moving were bold, then Elgar's last act before leaving Worcester was positively intrepid. He gave up every single one of his existing pupils. In his mind, a fresh start was needed – and it was surely to be found in London. It was an admirable burst of optimism, coinciding with a much more "get up and go" attitude from Elgar. In fact, armed with a copy of his recently composed piece for violin and piano, *Liebesgruss*, he decided to roam the publishing streets of London, determined to make himself and his new wife some money. In the end, Schott bought the work for two guineas. They eventually released it under the French version of the title, *Salut d'Amour*, and it soon became Elgar's first "hit". Sadly, Elgar had sold it to Schott as a buy-out and he earned no royalties. So, despite the fact that it fairly flew out of the music shops – in four different arrangements – Elgar still made just his original fee of £5. Eventually, some considerable time later, Schott relented and paid Elgar a royalty.

The happy couple honeymooned in Ventnor, on the Isle of Wight. The island was rather en vogue at the time, largely due to the fact that Queen Victoria had had Osborne House house built there, in the style of an Italian villa, with stunning landscaped gardens. The Elgars stayed somewhere altogether less grand. In fact, if you visit the Isle of Wight today, and head for the very end of the esplanade in Ventnor, make sure to look upwards when you are wending along the rather steep Alexandra Gardens. Just to the side of the window, on a rather imposing, bay-fronted, four-storey mansion is a plaque which records, simply *"Sir Edward Elgar, composer, stayed here in 1889"*.

Back in London, the Elgars hit reality with a bump. Elgar himself had very little money. Alice had a small income and this was put to good use in allowing them to listen to some of the amazing musical concerts available in the capital at the time.

When Elgar Was 32 . . .

They heard Brahms's *Symphony No.3*, the *Symphonic Variations* by Dvořák, and part of Wagner's *Götterdämmerung*, as well as Rossini's *William Tell* and Verdi's *Othello,* which was by then still only two years old.

Over the summer, they moved back to Alice's house, Saetermo, in Malvern, to enjoy an idyllic season of music-making with friends – and some composing. Elgar began to jot down some initial thoughts for a cantata, based on Henry Longfellow's translation of Ludwig Uhland's *"Der schwarze Ritter"*, which translates as *"The Black Knight"*. With newly married optimistic zeal, he decided that the work would be on a large and ground-breaking scale, with a greater role for the orchestra than almost any cantata before it. Indeed, it could be seen as a type of choral symphony – or at least a symphonic choral work.

When summer had been and gone, Elgar and Alice moved back to London, but this time to Upper Norwood, to stay at the home of Alice's cousin, William, at his house, Oaklands, on what is now Fountains Drive. These days, with the London transport system favouring, as it does, the north, Norwood might not seem a particularly obvious place for a music-lover. In those days, of course, with the amazing Crystal Palace providing many of the capital's concerts, it was a perfect place for Elgar. He had his own grand piano and organ installed in the house and even had his father come down from Worcester to do the tuning.

These early days must have been quite exciting for Elgar. By way of icing on the cake of a great year, he began to achieve a few more performances of his music. *Salut d'Amour* was played particularly often, including a performance at the Crystal Palace, courtesy of August Manns. He was also getting the odd thing published, too – his *Eleven Vesper Voluntaries*, for example. Was he beginning to make it, aged 32, as a composer? Quite possibly. Around November time, he received news that was to be the cherry on top of that icing – a commission from the Three Choirs Festival.

The year 1890 started as 1889 had ended – with great news. Alice was pregnant. The couple moved out of Alice's cousin's house and into 51 Avonmore Road, West Kensington, with Alice selling her pearls so that they could afford it. As the bump got bigger, Elgar began work on the Worcester commission. An entry in his diary in May reveals what he had chosen to be at the heart of the new piece:

Commenced Froissart.

Jean Froissart was the 14th-century author of *The Chronicles of Chivalry.*

When Elgar Was 33 . . .

Elgar worked on the score of *Froissart,* which was to be a concert overture for orchestra. It was finished by July and Elgar was encouraged that Novello's accepted it for publication. It pleased him less that he had to hand over the copyright to the work as a condition of publication. A month later, on 14 August, Alice gave birth to a daughter, whom they christened Carice Irene Elgar. She was baptized shortly afterwards at Brook Green's ornate, neo-gothic Catholic Church.

Rehearsals of *Froissart* got under way in Worcester in August. Elgar's father attended. The premiere was in the Public Hall, Worcester, in September. The critics were encouraging, believing that the work showed off

How To Compose Like Elgar

OK, first things first – we can't give you instructions on how to compose like Elgar. Or if we did, it would start something like "Step 1: Become a musical genius . . ." and so on. What we can do, however, is tell you Elgar's methods.

Composers work in many different ways. Mozart, for example, very often spent entire day-long journeys working out music in his head. When he arrived at his destination, the actual act of composing had often been done en route, and the part with the paper and pen was almost just copying it out, from his head.

Elgar was different. He kept musical notebooks in which he would write down ANYTHING that came into his head: sections of harmony, tunes, scraps of ideas on how to get from one tune to another – anything. No musical thought went to waste. He would also improvise at the piano – there are

Elgar's potential. Significantly for Elgar, too, a 20-year-old man called Ivor Atkins was at that time both an Oxford music undergraduate and the assistant organist at Hereford Cathedral. He rushed to Elgar's dressing room after the concert, overwhelmed by what he had heard. Atkins would go on to be a famed editor of music, the head of the Royal College of Organists and was, eventually, knighted for his services to music. For now, though, he had simply become one of Elgar's biggest fans and friends.

recordings, in fact, of his doing this later in life. Often it was after a long day teaching and he would simply improvise tunes on the piano.

Occasionally Alice, his wife, would shout an approving comment (this is exactly how the Enigma Variations *were born). Then, when he either received a commission or wanted to work on a new piece for his own benefit, he would need peace and quiet – a woodland setting seemed to bring out the best in him – and would look to combine current thoughts in his head with selected materials from his books. He would compose a piano version first and then, often after an interval, work on converting the piano version for full orchestra – this last part a particular forte of Elgar's.*

Sometimes, particularly later on in life, Elgar would be using tunes and sections from his notebooks which were years old. Nothing went to waste!

Alice wasn't able to be there at the premiere of *Froissart,* as she was still weak from childbirth – one of the few times Carice would come between Alice and Elgar, or Elgar's music. Elgar himself was said to be finding his new social circle, much of it Alice's social circle, rather novel. Some accounts at the time report that Elgar had taken almost to dressing as a country squire.

Although the early signs had been good, Elgar was, nevertheless, finding life as a jobbing composer very hard. As a particularly bad winter drew in, Elgar succumbed to the pressures of making a musical living. He became unwell, something that was not helped by his decision to begin teaching violin again. While he didn't regret having given up all his pupils some 18 months earlier, it did mean finding a complete set of new ones. He took a job teaching at a private girls' school called The Mount, in Malvern, run by a woman who was to become a close family friend and seemingly permanent baby-sitter to Carice, Rosa Burley.

Across the winter and early spring of 1891, Elgar found the travelling hard. The teaching in Malvern was effectively a musical catch-22: it brought the money that Elgar needed to be able to continue composing, but it also took up the bulk of his time, preventing him from composing. After braving it out for some months, the Elgars took a decision.

When Elgar Was 34 . . .

In March 1891, the Elgars moved out of London, renting for a short time until they moved into a semi-detached house in Malvern Link, with a shared garden and tennis court. They called it Forli, after the Italian renaissance painter, Melozzo da Forli, who, much in the same way as had been the case with the composer Palestrina, was named after the small town from which he originated, namely Forli, near Ravenna. Sections of his angelic frescoes can still be seen in the Vatican Museum.

Somewhat bruised and beaten by his first, failed
attempt to conquer London, Elgar settled once again
into life in Malvern. Although he was said to be not
the most patient teacher in the world, he buckled
down to the rigours of daily peripatetic teaching,
becoming good friends with Rosa Burley in the
process. He bought himself a Nicolo Gagliano violin
from a rather posh music shop, Hills of Bond Street,
which inspired him to write another small piece for
violin and piano, *La Capriceuse*.

Elgar celebrated the New Year of 1892 in style, at
the home of Alice's friend, William Baker. Baker
was almost exactly the same age as Elgar – born just
a few months later – but their lives were very
different. He had inherited Hasfield Court when he
was 18 and the Elgars were frequent guests at the
historic house. No doubt the history of the
building, which was the ancestral home of the
Pauncefoote family up until the 16th century,
would have struck a chord with Elgar's current
passion for Froissart, Forli and all things from this
age of chivalry. In addition, he found that he and
William Baker shared a common enthusiasm for the
music of Wagner.

Despite the strain of continued teaching – he added
Worcester Girls' High School to his roster – Elgar
managed to work through the first few months
of the year on *The Black Knight*, to the point
where he was able to play some of the music,

in sketch form, to the assistant organist from Worcester, Hugh Blair. Blair, who also worked as the conductor of the Worcester Festival Chorus, was impressed enough to promise that the Worcester Festival would perform the new work, when it was completed.

Lovers of Elgar's gorgeous *Serenade for Strings* might be interested to know that this famous work hails from this period too. It was around now that Elgar reworked one of his earlier scores – the *Three Pieces for Strings* – into what we now know as the *Serenade*. In a manner reminiscent of the Fred Astaire screen test report which allegedly said:

Can't sing. Can't act. Balding. Can dance a little.

the publishers, Novello & Co., refused to publish the *Serenade for Strings*, branding it:

Unsaleable.

It continues to be one of his most popular works even now, more than 100 years later. Although we do have the benefit of hindsight, it is still remarkable to think of someone rejecting a work which so clearly has all the hallmarkings of the classic "Elgar sound".

When Elgar Was 35 . . .

An extended trip to the continent afforded Elgar the time to see some wonderful music at Bayreuth and beyond. He managed to watch Wagner's *Parsifal* a couple of times, as well as *Tristan and Isolde* and *Die Meistersinger*. In Bonn, he took time to visit 20 Bongasse, Beethoven's birthplace, no doubt struck by the tiny attic room in which one of his favourite composers was born. Other places included on the itinerary were Cologne and Nuremburg, as well as Munich and Heidelberg – the last two giving him musical food for thought when it came to writing his six songs, *"From the Bavarian Highlands"*, some four years later.

Back on English soil, there was good news from a German publisher, Breitkopf and Härtel, who had agreed to publish the *Serenade for Strings*.

By September, Elgar had finished work on *The Black Knight*. Novello, no doubt thinking of the extensive Victorian tradition of both music festivals AND grand cantatas and oratorios for those festivals, accepted the new work for publication. Elgar ended the year somewhat buoyed and allowed himself the luxury of improving his golf. A friend of a friend of Alice's, Richard Baxter Townshend, taught him the finer points over Christmas, and the Elgars ended the year happy.

It was April 1893 before Elgar's next significant musical milestone. As well as a premiere of his vocal piece, *"Spanish Serenade"*, Hugh Blair kept his word with a Worcester Festival Chorus performance of *The Black Knight*, with Elgar on the conductor's rostrum.

When Elgar Was 36 . . .

What do you buy a 36-year-old composer for his birthday? In 1893, Elgar received a copy of the vocal score of Wagner's *Tristan*, which no doubt stirred some pining for the German composer's music. By August, Elgar was back in Munich for a Wagner Festival, taking in a whole host of the master's operas: *Die Meistersinger*, *The Ring* Cycle, *Tristan* and *Tannhäuser*.

Towards the end of the year, having returned to Malvern, Elgar's thoughts once again switched to the violin, but not just in terms of teaching. He sought out an old violin sonata from some years back and began reworking it. This method of returning to old pieces and rethinking them was one that would stay with Elgar all his life. As late as 1931, when he was 74, he was reworking older pieces into new ones. This time, though, in 1893, an old violin sonata became a brass, organ and strings piece called *Sursum Corda*. (*Sursum Corda* is a phrase from the Catholic Church, a short Latin verse meaning "lift up your hearts".)

In early 1894, and heartened by the fairly positive reception of *The Black Knight* in Worcester, Elgar began work on a new cantata, to be called *Scenes from the Saga of King Olaf*. By this time, it may be worth pointing out, that Grieg's saga-based work, *Peer Gynt*, was around 20 years old. Indeed, only months earlier, Grieg had visited England to receive his honorary degree from Cambridge University – at the instigation of its one-time professor of music, C. V. Stanford. Elgar's particularly English-Victorian interpretation saw him turn, for his take on sagas, to Longfellow and his version of *The Saga of King Olaf*. Just around the same time as his *Sursum Corda* was being played for the Duke of York's visit to Worcester, Elgar began to write the first few sketches for this new cantata.

When Elgar Was 37 . . .

The summer was whiled away in idyllic style, once again. Not until the Edwardian summers of the early 1900s would the Elgars be as happy as this. Their time was spent entertaining guests, visiting other people's homes, and playing golf with friends. Soon afterwards, they were back in Germany again, leaving Carice with Rosa Burley for the first of many such occasions. They visited Garmisch and Munich, hearing performances of the by now obligatory Wagner operas. They even found time to visit Goethe's house in Frankfurt.

Behind Every Good Man . . .

When you examine the role of Alice Elgar in her husband's life, it's possible to put forward an argument that Elgar was, in fact, working in a partnership. Not only was Alice famous for being his driving force, pushing him to compose and boosting him when reviews were poor, she was also responsible for more of Elgar's music than she is often given credit for.

First, she made up his manuscript paper for him. To explain: music manuscript paper in those days came in pure blank form – just one big page with lots and lots of musical staves on it. Alice would rule off the sections for different instruments, or instrumental groupings, effectively making a "template" for Elgar to fill in as he composed. She would help out on instrumentation and even put Elgar's bar lines in for him. These are the lines that separate one section of music from another. If you then add in the number of times Elgar set Alice's actual poems to music, then her role begins to look not so much that of a supportive wife, but more a partner in a cottage industry.

The Elgars returned to Garmisch the following summer, managing to fit in a visit to see the *Flying Dutchman* in Munich. Elgar had already spent the early part of 1895 thinking about his brand new commission. It was to be for the Worcester Festival, and he had more than a year to write it. Not surprisingly, they wanted a choral work and Elgar had decided upon a story from the bible, in which a blind man is given back his sight by Jesus. It was to be called *Lux Christi* – The Light of Christ.

When Elgar Was 38 . . .

The Worcester commission was soon followed by another from the North Staffordshire Festival, although this came without a fee. Nevertheless, at this stage in Elgar's career, a large public performance was not to be sniffed at and he readily agreed. Besides, he had already begun *King Olaf* and this would fit the bill nicely. Elgar worked at quite a pace on both new works, well into the new year, completing *King Olaf* by February, and *Lux Christi* by April. Neither work would remain as Elgar had originally intended, with his publisher asking both for cuts in *King Olaf* and for *Lux Christi* to change its name to *The Light of Life*. The reason for the latter request was just in case its Catholic resonances might offend any more Establishment Church of England sensibilities.

When Elgar Was 39 . . .

As the spring of 1896 turned to summer, Elgar orchestrated both pieces, occasionally working in a tent in his garden. By the September and October respectively, *The Light of Life* and *King Olaf* were ready for their premieres. These two events could not have been more different.

The Light of Life was well received, with even the Master of the Queen's Music, Sir Walter Parratt, present at one of the rehearsals. *King Olaf*, on the other hand, was very nearly a bit of a mess. By all accounts, the tenor didn't know his part well enough. Elgar, who had spent the afternoon watching his beloved football club, Wolverhampton Wanderers, playing at home, was conducting.

Perhaps Wolves made Elgar a little distracted, as they weren't having their best season ever. They had been beaten in the FA Cup Final and ended up finishing 14th in their league. Elgar was said to have lost control of his orchestra – to the extent that the leader, the chief violinist, was forced to jump to his feet and beat time, wildly and desperately, with his bow.

Despite its ignominious birth, *King Olaf* turned out to be the more successful of the pieces, taken up by many of the thriving choral societies of the time. Many critics also recognized that, despite the problems with its premiere, Olaf was not so much a king as a messenger for Elgar – loudly presaging what was to come from his pen in the future.

The year 1897 saw Queen Victoria's Diamond Jubilee. Although the country did not yet know it, it was also probably the high point of empire, with things starting to roll downhill from there. The Boer War, with its near international humiliation for Britain, and then the First World War, would soon become two appalling signposts on the declining

Nimrod, The Mighty Jaeger

Elgar found himself in luck when his publishers, Novello, appointed a new man to be his point of contact. He was Augustus J. Jaeger, born in Düsseldorf in 1854, but resident in England since 1878. Interestingly enough, for a man whose image has become muddied with jingoism and flag-waving, Elgar was immediately more respectful of Jaeger because he was German. Elgar loved the German classical music tradition. From the start, the two hit it off, with Jaeger understanding Elgar's music, realizing how special it was, and yet, at the same time, never afraid to push him to improve it. These are the perfect skills for any editor. Jaeger and Elgar became close friends and, of course, he was accorded perhaps one of the greatest honours in all music by being cast as Nimrod – *the supreme section of the* Enigma Variations *and one of the world's favourite pieces of classical music of all time. More of that later. Jaeger lived in the Muswell Hill area of London and, if you are ever in the neighbourhood, you can see a plaque on his house at 37 Curzon Road.*

curve of this once far-reaching realm. In 1897, things didn't seem so bad, though. Queen Victoria had become Britain's longest serving monarch, surpassing her grandfather, King George III. The prime ministers of all the self-governing colonies were invited to London for a special series of events, culminating in a huge, triumphal procession for the septuagenarian queen, who was by now wheelchair-bound. In the world of literature, Rudyard Kipling penned his poem, *Recessional* – itself full of foreboding for the empire, and Sir Arthur Conan Doyle included a reference to the Diamond Jubilee in one of his Sherlock Holmes books.

For his part, Elgar wrote two works: the fittingly entitled *Imperial March* and a cantata, *The Banner of St George*. He had completed the march late the previous year and it was premiered at a Crystal Palace concert in March 1897. As a sign of Elgar's creeping acceptance by the musical establishment, though, it was also played both for a special Diamond Jubilee Royal Garden Party in June and at the Albert Hall some time later. *The Banner of St George*, described as a ballad for chorus and orchestra, was premiered in London in May.

When Elgar Was 40 . . .

Not long after that, Elgar started to exchange letters with his new editor at Novello, August Jaeger. It soon dawned on Elgar that he now had a friend within his publishing company, and one with sufficient musical ability to be able occasionally to steer Elgar's music in very much the right direction. One of his oft-quoted letters, from the very beginning of their correspondence, shows Elgar starting to appreciate his new-found friend. He is talking about particularly heartfelt sections of his music when he says:

I always say to my wife . . . if you cut that, it would bleed . . . You seem to see that.

No year around this period of Elgar's life would have been complete without its trip to Germany and, by August, the Elgars were back in Bavaria once again. This time, they also managed to meet one of Elgar's favourite composers, Richard Strauss, after a performance of Wagner's *Tristan* in Munich.

The year ended positively yet fairly uneventfully: Elgar's *Te Deum* and *Benedictus* were premiered in Hereford, with his new chum Jaeger showing up in support. Elgar also managed to sell his small violin-and-piano piece *Evensong* to Novello for a much needed 10 guineas. They changed the title to *Chanson de Nuit*. Money-wise, Elgar wasn't doing too badly. He and Alice were surviving but, as he told Jaeger in a letter, his money was not yet coming from his compositions. Had he had to rely solely on composing in 1897, he would have had only £86 to live on – that's the equivalent of around £6,500 today. The rest came from teaching and, increasingly, conducting. The new Worcestershire Philharmonic Orchestra was founded at the end of 1897, and it immediately appointed Elgar as its conductor.

The year 1898 continued as 1897 had ended: positively. The January post brought a commission from the Leeds Festival floating onto his doormat at Forli. They wanted yet another cantata, of course. Elgar may have been desperate to develop his orchestral style. After all he was 40 years old and could no longer be considered a spring chicken. However, the dominant festival circuit of Victorian England was crying out for cantatas and oratorios, to feed its thriving choral communities. So a cantata it was. All Elgar needed was the subject matter – and on one of his long walks in the Worcestershire countryside, he found it – and more.

On one particularly beautiful walk, he and Alice came across an especially glorious view which framed one particular hill quite magnificently. Alice immediately began encouraging Elgar to use the sight as inspiration for a story. Within a few weeks, he had the idea of the story of *Caractacus* ready in his head as the subject for his Leeds cantata. Another of his walks, though, around the same time, yielded up something much more tangible. Having tramped deep into a woodland area, Elgar came across an old gamekeeper's cottage, not far from Storridge. Its setting and exquisite views struck him immediately. He had always recognized that he was simply able to compose better if he was seated in front of a view of his favourite Worcestershire hills and valleys. Within weeks, the Elgars had rented the cottage, which was called Birchwood Lodge, and, by summer, Elgar was ensconced with his manuscript paper and his views, writing *Caractacus*. He composed like a man inspired

and, as he finished each section, he sent it to Leeds
for them to rehearse.

When Elgar Was 41 . . .

By June, the piece was finished in outline. By
August, it was completely orchestrated, and sealed
with a dedication to Queen Victoria. Over the late
summer months, members of the Leeds Festival
Chorus were taken through their parts by their
choirmaster, until it was ready for rehearsals in the
autumn. Would it prove to be as shaky and unsteady
a premiere as had *King Olaf*, just two years earlier?

The late omens were good. The successful English
composers Hubert Parry and Arthur Sullivan were
to be festival conductors. The composer Fauré, who
had also written a piece for the festival, was present
at the final rehearsal at the start of October.

At the premiere, four days later in the Town Hall,
the audience thought the work was fantastic.
Indeed, the chorus, who had given an excellent
performance, gave Elgar a standing ovation. One
critic wrote that it was:

. . . a triumph and everybody admitted it . . .

Sadly, the other critics must have been at a different
concert. The overwhelming opinion of the main
body of professional opinion-givers was negative.

Elgar left Leeds bloodied but unbowed. Indeed, from out of the maelstrom of bad notices, standing ovations and stunning choral singing that was the premiere of *Caractacus*, Elgar would turn to the piece that would change the course of his life.

Immediately after the first performance of *Caractacus*, Elgar returned to Worcestershire and began to sketch some ideas . . . for a set of variations.

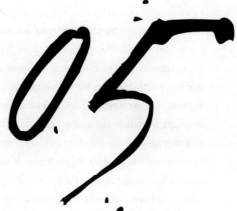

Edward Elgar:
Superstar

Back in Worcestershire, the same Elgar who was
given a standing ovation by the Leeds Festival
Chorus returned to teaching violin to his various
local pupils in order to make ends meet. After one
particularly laborious day – the date is well
documented, it was 21 October, 1898 – Elgar
arrived home and had dinner with Alice. After a
relaxing post-prandial cigar, he retired to the piano
and began to play.

When she heard one particular "doodle" on the
keys, Alice shouted in from the other room to ask
him to repeat what he'd just played, and he did. At

this point, she asked him what it was. He is said to have replied:

Oh, it's nothing – but something might be made of it.

Elgar spent much of the rest of the evening playing the same little tune to his wife, only in the style of various of their mutual friends, each time changing the tune to match either the character of the person or some recollected incident in their friendship. Little more was said about the tune. It was only a tune at this point and not a piece. Nevertheless, Alice had been present at the birth of the piece that would change both their lives – what was to become the *Variations on an Original Theme*, otherwise known as *The Enigma Variations*.

Other musical ideas vied for attention from the 41-year-old composer. He still harboured intentions to write a symphony in tribute to the life of General Gordon.

Also, the Norwich Festival stepped in towards the end of the year, with a request for a new piece for the promising and increasingly popular 25-year-old alto, Clara Butt. Nevertheless, this idea of a set of variations based on his friends was still bubbling away inside him. It would not be forgotten.

In the January of 1899, and having accepted the commission from Norwich, Elgar travelled to

London to see Clara Butt. Butt had been born in Southwick in Sussex in 1873 but was now living at 7 Harley Road, in Hampstead. Bizarrely, when Elgar arrived, the singer was in the bath and refused to see him. A few days later, after a serendipitous word of complaint to her manager, Elgar had to repeat the visit, this time successfully managing to meet Miss Butt and show her the first drafts of the work that she was to premiere at that year's Norwich Festival. It was called *Sea Pictures*.

And that "serendipitous" word of complaint? Well, it fell on the ears of one Nat Vert, Butt's manager at the time. He also happened to be the agent for one of the world's foremost conductors, Hans Richter. Elgar talked to Vert about the set of variations that he was composing, each one a portrait of a friend. He asked the well-connected Vert if he would agree to ask Richter to conduct a first performance of them, at one of his many concerts. When Vert agreed to the approach, Elgar nervously wrote to Jaeger, asking him not to let on that Richter was to be asked – just in case he said "No".

By February, the variations were finished, and apart from his *Chanson de Matin,* the companion piece to his *Chanson de Nuit,* this was more or less the last full piece that Elgar was to write at Forli. By March, the Elgars had moved to a large, detached house in Wells Road, Great Malvern. Elgar, in an apt display of his love of mysterious wordplay – this was the

time of the "Enigma", after all – named the house
Craeg Lea: an anagram of the letters E, A, C Elgar.
(Edward, Alice and Carice). The new house, with
its first-floor writing room, complete with views
across the Severn Valley, must have brought them a
wave of good luck. Almost simultaneously, Elgar
heard the news that Hans Richter had agreed to
conduct the premiere of his new variations.

When Elgar Was 42 . . .

The *Variations on an Original Theme* were
premiered on 19 June, 1899. They proved to be a
triumph for Elgar, despite an argument with
Novello over whether they were willing to pay him
royalties. The *Enigma Variations* were met with
critical acclaim which, almost overnight, changed
the perception of Elgar from a provincial also-ran to
a national star and then, ultimately, to the potential
saviour of English music. Richter immediately took
the *Variations* on a tour, which spread Elgar's new-
found fame even further. Granville Bantock
conducted them in New Brighton, a popular
Victorian seaside resort on the Wirral. England, it
seemed, was waking up to the great composer on
its doorstep.

Elgar spent the stifling summer finishing *Sea
Pictures* for Clara Butt, ready for the October
premiere. *Sea Pictures* is often criticized for the
quality of the words within. Indeed, Elgar, in

general, is often criticized for the quality of the
words he chose to set, whether they be written by
Alice (one of her poems features in *Sea Pictures*) or
by folk such as Longfellow. Sometimes, we think,
this criticism is justified; on other occasions,
it may simply be a matter of material
becoming dated.

When the new century dawned, Elgar's position, as
a great composer who probably still had his greatest
works to come, was assured. He soon began to work
on a new commission from Birmingham. It was for
a grand choral work – but then, what else would
they ask for?

Elgar harked back to his old idea of
commemorating General Gordon in some way. To
satisfy the nature of the commission, however, Elgar
focussed instead on something that had been in
Gordon's possession when he was killed, namely
Newman's epic poem, *The Dream of Gerontius*,
complete with all his own notes and markings.
Elgar abridged the words himself and soon began
sketching out the music.

When Elgar Was 43 . . .

By June, Elgar had finished the first draft of
The Dream of Gerontius, and, as a result, allowed
himself to get to know Mr Phoebus a lot
better.

I Want To Ride My Bicycle . . .

In June 1900, Elgar took delivery of a Royal Sunbeam bicycle, for which he had paid £21.10s.0d – a phenomenal price, which equates to around £1,500 today. Elgar christened the bike "Mr Phoebus". It was another of his plays on words. Phoebus meant "radiant one" and was often applied to Apollo because of his connection to the sun. Elgar enjoyed many cycle rides with his friends and eventually upgraded to an even better bike, giving the Sunbeam to Jaeger. In the end, though, Elgar ditched the cycling, saying there were too many cars on the road.

1900 was more or less devoted to the choral work for Birmingham. However, when the time of the premiere arrived, in October, the stage was set for another disaster. This was the real thing, though, and not just the near-disaster that was *King Olaf*.

The finished work, *The Dream of Gerontius*, is, as any chorus member will tell you, a big sing. It is a complex and tough work that needs careful, musical and meticulous preparation. To be fair, Elgar had been quite close to the wire when it came to delivering the score of *The Dream of Gerontius* to Novello & Co., who were then, in turn, late in getting the printed parts to the chorus. When the concert arrived, the singers were not in a prime state of readiness, to say the least. The concert was a well-documented shambles. Nevertheless, although Elgar himself felt downcast about it the following morning, the critics had seen through the poor performance and hailed the piece as a work of genius. One even said that his mere printed review could not do justice to such a great work.

Elgar's "overnight sensation" reputation was lasting well into "the following day". The *Enigma Variations* and now *The Dream of Gerontius* had made him the most sought-after composer in the land. Later in the year, Cambridge University offered Elgar an honorary doctorate, which he nearly refused to accept, on account of money worries. His fears that he could not even afford to buy the robes to wear while he accepted his degree were, however, eventually dispelled, when a friend loaned him the money. Fittingly, on St Cecilia's Day 1900, he was awarded his degree in Cambridge.

With England now at the height of its commitment to the Boer War, Elgar began work on a new march. He was also commissioned by the Philharmonic Society (now the Royal Philharmonic Society) to come up with an orchestral work. At last, the orchestral commission he had been yearning for! Inspired by a visit to London, where he had been to the famous Guildhall, amongst other places, he began work on a concert overture, too.

By the January of the following year, though, there was one particular tune from the new march that he could not get out of his head. One of his letters to Jaeger contains the immortal line:

Gosh, man, I've got a tune in my head.

Nevertheless, as the country came to terms with the death of Queen Victoria, Elgar completed his concert overture for the Philharmonic Society in March, and named it after a derivation of the old word for London, calling it the *Cockaigne Overture*.

Almost immediately, though, he was back at work on the tune that had been nagging away in his head – the march. Again, convinced that he was on to a great thing, he wrote in his letters:

I've got a tune that will knock 'em flat . . . A tune that comes around once in a lifetime.

And he was right. The tune he was talking about was the one that we now know more commonly as *"Land of Hope and Glory"*. When he'd finished it, though, in 1901, it was still known simply as a part of his march, *Pomp and Circumstance March No. 1*.

When Elgar Was 44 . . .

The *Cockaigne Overture* was premiered in June 1901 and Elgar retired to Birchwood for the summer, in preparation for the October premiere

in Liverpool, not only of the *Pomp and
Circumstance March No. 1,* but also of its partner,
the *Pomp and Circumstance March No. 2.* Henry
Wood played them shortly afterwards in one of his
Promenade Concerts, whereupon the reception for
No. 1 was staggering.

The people simply rose and yelled . . .

he wrote, adding that he had to repeat the march
twice before the crowd would allow him to move on
to *No. 2.* A legend had been born.

By early 1902, the same musical world that had
prepared for the Queen's Diamond Jubilee
Celebrations in 1897 now readied itself for the
coronation of her son, the soon to be Edward VII.
For the Diamond Jubilee, Elgar provided the
Imperial March and *The Banner of St George.* This
time, his contribution to the national events would
be all the more memorable.

Meanwhile, *The Dream of Gerontius* was continuing
to take Elgar's name far and wide. In Düsseldorf, it
went down a storm with Germany's greatest living
composer, Richard Strauss, more or less declaring
the end of the one-time "land without music". He
asked people to celebrate:

*. . . the welfare and success of the first English
progressivist, Meister Edward Elgar.*

Around about May, Elgar was sent words by A. C. Benson, a teacher at Eton School, which he set as a celebratory piece for Edward VII, the *Coronation Ode*. However, for the last section of the ode, Elgar had reworked the "tune that will knock 'em flat" especially for the nation's favourite alto, Clara Butt.

When Elgar Was 45 . . .

By the time of the June Coronation Concert, Butt was performing the last section of the *Coronation Ode* separately, as a song in its own right. *"Land of Hope and Glory"* swept the nation. Many predicted that Elgar's musical achievements would be marked in the Honours List for 1902. They considered it scandalous when he was overlooked.

September saw Elgar once again spreading the word of *The Dream of Gerontius*, this time with a slightly "expurgated" version, free from references to purgatory, for fear of offence. At the Worcester Festival, he is said to have conducted the work with tears streaming down his face, full of thoughts of the recent death of his mother at the age of 80.

His mother's death may or may not have been a significant factor in raising the importance of a seemingly inconsequential meeting in October that year. At the Sheffield Festival, Elgar was introduced, via a friend of a friend, to a women who was the wife of a local MP, Charles Stuart-Wortley, and the daughter of the English pre-Raphaelite painter, John Everett Millais. After that perfunctory handshake of a meeting in Sheffield, Alice Stuart-Wortley would go on to become one of the most influential women in Elgar's life.

It was another good year all in all, despite its ups and downs, ending with Elgar beginning to put together the wherewithal for the libretto to a new work. It was another hefty choral piece, based on the lives of the Apostles.

Rule, Britannica!

For Christmas in 1902, Elgar was sent something rather special – a complete set of the 10th edition of the Encyclopaedia Britannica *in its own specially made revolving bookcase. Elgar quickly became besotted with it, looking up anything and everything he could get his hands on and even writing a poem on the subject:*

I know the height of Ararat,
Specific gravity of fat,
And heaps of other things besides,
As what makes vermin scratch their hides!

He showed the bookcase off, proudly, to Jaeger when he visited. Alice eventually had to send it away, worried that his "endless revolving" of it would distract him from his work on The Apostles.

By March 1903, Elgar had progressed from merely having a set of words to *The Apostles* to having completed a substantial part of the music.

When Elgar Was 46 . . .

The first performance of *The Dream of Gerontius* in the capital was on 6 June, 1903 and it went well, although it did distract Elgar somewhat from his new work, *The Apostles*. Nevertheless, by the time October came round, Birmingham Town Hall was full. Hundreds of people were turned away from the premiere. It is a mark of how Elgar's fortunes had changed so quickly. Not much more than a couple of years previously, an Elgar premiere meant relatively little. Now, they could sell it several times over. *The Apostles* did not disappoint its huge, first night audience, either, with Hans Richter declaring it:

. . . the greatest work since Beethoven's Mass in D minor.

The money from his arrangement with Novello for *The Apostles* provided a much-needed financial fillip in the fading weeks of 1903. The Elgars put some of it to immediate good use with a trip to Italy. They rented a house in Alassio, in the south of the country, without the now 13-year-old Carice. Holidays, it has to be said, were generally spent without Carice, who was usually shipped off to stay with Rosa Burley. At Christmas time, however, the Elgars relented and had Carice join them for a short time. Elgar, for his part, began work on a small concert overture, named after their holiday destination, *In the South (Alassio)*, and filled with influences picked up throughout their stay. Visitors today to the place where they stayed, Alassio, are reminded of the city's musical connections when they walk down a street called "via Edward Elgar".

Carice Elgar

By the standards of today, Carice Elgar can come across as a slightly sad child, who was often left with family friends while her mother and father went off on holiday. Her frequent minder, Rosa Burley, described her as "permanently sad". Was it just a typical childhood in a period when youngsters were seen but not heard? Or was it something more? Will we ever know? When Elgar was long gone, she perhaps gave some clue, saying that she knew all the people commemorated in the Enigma Variations *and "didn't like any of them". Had she just forgotten that her father and mother were both themselves variations?*

Elgar stayed on at Alassio well into the January of 1904, returning to England partly to fulfil an obligation to dine with King Edward VII at Marlborough House.

By February, he had completed the orchestral work started in Italy, *In the South (Alassio)*. It would go on to form part of a remarkable festival in March. But this wasn't a Birmingham Festival, a Leeds Festival, or even a Three Choirs Festival. As another mark of the amazing change in Elgar's public standing, the man who had dined with the king earlier in the year was, in March, given his own festival. This was the Elgar Festival, a three-day celebration of the music of the greatest living English composer, held in London's Covent Garden.

A poster at the time promises:

Dr Hans Richter, having with his Manchester Orchestra and Chorus, devoted special attention to Dr Elgar's works, a perfect assemblage may be anticipated.

Certainly, the king and queen thought so, attending as they did for the first two days' concerts of *The Dream of Gerontius* and *The Apostles*, with the queen sufficiently impressed to stay on for the third day's performances of *Froissart*, *The Enigma Variations* and the new *In the South (Alassio)*.

After the Covent Garden Festival in March, Elgar was further cheered as the spring progressed. He became a member of the exclusive Athenaeum Club; he was awarded further degrees from Durham and Leeds Universities; and, possibly the crowning moment, he was knighted in June. Arise, Sir Edward Elgar!

We think it's fair to say that 1904 represented the high point of recognition of Elgar's musical achievement and reputation. Even though several major works were still to be written, Elgar would never again enjoy quite so much personal glory. Paradoxically, it could be argued that it was his greatest work of 1904 that would spell the beginning of of the gloomy downward curve – the great *Introduction and Allegro for Strings*.

When Elgar Was 47 . . .

A new knight needs a new house. So it was that Sir Edward Elgar moved into the "White House". "Plas Gwyn" is Welsh for "White House" and it stood around a mile outside Hereford. It was here that he added to his collection of *Pomp and Circumstance Marches*, penning No. 3 not long after he had moved in.

There were still two more pieces of good news to come in 1904, though. First, Elgar was to be the first Chair of Music at Birmingham University. This, in some respects, placed Elgar between a rock and a hard place in that the person putting up the money, one Richard Peyton, had made it clear that Elgar had been given first refusal on the Chair and that, should he turn it down, the endowment might not go ahead. It involved giving half a dozen lectures across the year. Elgar accepted, partly touched, partly fearful that the university would lose its money.

Second, the then newly formed London Symphony Orchestra had asked him to write them a brand new orchestral work. With an idea in his head already, Elgar began work on a piece for strings, but with a separate part for a string quartet – the work that would become the *Introduction and Allegro for Strings*. He was still working on it when it was announced that he was to receive yet another honorary degree, this time from Oxford University. He finished the new piece by February 1905, only just in time for its March premiere. This was quite a habit for Elgar and quite often in his career we find him only just finishing his commissions in time for them to be performed. Sometimes he was guilty of not leaving a big enough gap for the musicians to be able to practise sufficiently. This was definitely the case with the *Introduction and Allegro for Strings*, which is still, today, a fierce little work to get together.

Sadly, at the premiere, where it was given its first outing alongside the new *Pomp and Circumstance March No. 3*, most of the critics were just that – critical. Many of his friends considered it his best work, but that didn't seem to matter at the time. Some experts believe that this was a turning point in Elgar's life. Or, at the very least, it was a precursor to what happened to him when he presented the first of his lectures in Birmingham. It was entitled "A Future for English Music" and it gave many in English society at the time their first view of Elgar, the man. His friends had known his foibles, preferences and, some might say, prejudices for years, but for the public, this was a first. And it didn't go down well. Even many of his friends were said to be squirming in their seats in the audience, as Elgar delivered a series of digs at, variously, academics, people who didn't "play" music and, quite obviously, the composer C. V. Stanford, whom Elgar considered to be second rate. It must have been an excruciating afternoon.

When Elgar Was 48 . . .

In June, Yale became the first American university to recognize Elgar's merits with an honorary degree and Elgar, much against his better judgement, was persuaded to cross the Atlantic to receive it. It was a particularly steamy New York summer and a rather hot and bothered, unwell and ultimately grumpy Elgar didn't exactly endear himself to the natives when he told one American reporter:

Your national anthem is even worse than England's!

Back home, that year's Worcester Festival was a little more special. Elgar had been awarded the Freedom of Worcester by the city's Lord Mayor, who was

none other than Hubert Leicester, the one-time bassoonist in his "shed" ensemble (see page 33). In order to accept it, Elgar had to process from the Worcester Guildhall to the cathedral, wearing the robes from one of his many honorary degrees. He was able to pass by his father's music shop at 10 The High Street, whereupon he stopped to doff his cap to his now 83-year-old dad, who was watching from the upstairs window – too frail to attend. It must have been a moving moment for them both.

A chance reading of an article in October revealed to Elgar that he had a fan in the then 30-year-old Wunder-violinist Fritz Kreisler. Kreisler had re-started his career as a soloist only six years earlier, following a spell in the Austrian army, and had stated, on the record to a journalist, that he thought Elgar was an equal to Beethoven and Brahms and was in fact:

. . . the greatest living English composer . . .

Elgar was touched and immediately began mapping out ideas for a brand new work – for violin.

The year 1905 ended much as had 1904, with the LSO. This time, it was a conducting tour with the new orchestra, although it was interspersed with new lectures for Birmingham, each one stirring up a hornets' nest all of its own as it was reported. Mind you, with titles such as "English Composers" or "Critics", Elgar was not exactly steering himself away from controversial ground.

In 1906, Elgar began work on the second part of what was always planned as *The Apostles* trilogy, a new oratorio eventually named *The Kingdom*. The words were culled from the Bible by Elgar himself. He worked hard on it for the first few months of the year, feeling the unforgiving weight of the deadlines on his shoulders. With the work only half finished, he and Alice set sail for America, where he was being further honoured. This time, rather than an honorary degree, it was with an astonishing eight-week-long Elgar Festival. This marathon event happened in Cincinnati, of all places. Sadly, on his very first day on American soil, he was devastated by the news that his father had died a couple of days earlier in Worcester. Distraught, he nevertheless pressed on with the US tour. This state of affairs might excuse, to some extent, his surly attitude to the Cincinnati press, a body of journalists who came to dislike this composer they regarded as a typically reserved and bad-tempered Englishman. Elgar, for his part, was keen to simply see out his US tour, including lunch with Andrew Carnegie at his home, and get back to his beloved English Edwardian idyll. And, of course, to finish *The Kingdom*.

When Elgar Was 49 . . .

By July he had done the job, at least in first draft form. He worked on the orchestral score throughout the high summer, stopping only for a trip to Aberdeen to pick up, yes, another honorary degree. The "bad news" year continued, though, in September with his brave friend, Jaeger, now struggling to both work and cope with the tuberculosis that had been diagnosed a couple of years earlier. By now, it had become touch and go as to whether Jaeger would be Elgar's man at Novello for much longer.

One shaft of light, though, was the premiere in October of *The Kingdom*. The critics appeared to approve.

January 1907 began with a holiday in Italy. The Elgars visited Naples, Capri and Rome, managing a trip to the Vatican while in the capital. They weren't back home for long, before Elgar was up and off again, this time for another mini-US tour. Travelling alone, Elgar oversaw a performance of *The Apostles* at New York's Carnegie Hall, as well as the American premiere of *The Kingdom*. Chicago, meanwhile, was treated to the *Enigma Variations*.

When Elgar Was 50 . . .

A wave of childhood nostalgia seemed to overcome
Elgar upon reaching his half century. He had lost
both his mother and father within the last five years
and this may have been a spur for him to look out
some distant childhood pieces that he had written
for him and his brothers and sisters to perform to
their parents. He set out to score them maturely, as
it were, with the benefit of his 50 years' experience.
They soon became a pair of orchestral suites, aptly
entitled *The Wand of Youth*.

This was also the year he plucked up the courage to
write to the Irish poet, Arthur O'Shaughnessy,
asking for permission to set to music his poem,
"The Music Makers". He had had the idea in his
head for some time, but the especially nostalgic feel
of 1907 had finally driven him to make the
approach. The poem would become the
centre-point of a piece in which he famously
quoted many of his earlier tunes. The words
also seem particularly apt for a man such
as Elgar:

We are the music makers,
*   We are the dreamers of dreams,*
Wandering by the lone sea-breakers,
*   And sitting by desolate streams;*
World losers and world-forsakers,
*   On whom the pale moon gleams:*

93

We are the movers and shakers
  Of the world for ever, it seems.

Elgar's Ark

Elgar was a frustrated scientist. All his life, he was attracted to chemistry in particular and, when he moved into Plas Gwyn, he had a shed converted into his own little chemical laboratory, which he called The Ark. Whenever he had the time, he would retire to The Ark to conduct his own experiments. He had some success and he patented his own hydrogen machine, called "Elgar's Sulphuretted Hydrogen Machine", which eventually went into manufacture. It wasn't always so successful a hobby, though. On one occasion, he caused an explosion that is said to have attracted all the dogs from the surrounding area when it blew up his water butt. Elgar staggered from The Ark and sat for a while to smoke his pipe. When one neighbour came running out to see what all the fuss was about, Elgar remained enigmatically tight-lipped on the cause of the chaos.

In November, Elgar left Britain to spend a full six months in Italy. He was ill with flu, in Rome, in early 1908; he saw Puccini operas in Florence; and he worked on what he was then calling his string quartet, but which eventually produced much of the musical heart of both his *Symphony No. 1* and the autobiographical *The Music Makers*.

Back home by May, the promising Italian winter
and spring was followed by a productive English
summer. He really and truly had the composing bug
once again and was working at a pace not seen since
perhaps the electric spring of 1898, and the work
on *Caractacus*. This time, though, his labours were
being directed not towards a pre-determined
commission for chorus, but to his own yearnings
for a particular type of pure, orchestral music –
"absolute" music, as he had put it in one of his
Birmingham lectures.

When Elgar Was 51 . . .

By August 1908, Elgar had resigned his
professorship at Birmingham in order to
concentrate on his new, absolute music. He retired
to a summer house that belonged to a friend called
Frank Schuster. It was affectionately called The Hut
and sat on the Thames at Bray, near Maidenhead.
He worked on the fourth and final movement of his
Symphony No. 1. By September, it was finished, and
dedicated to Hans Richter, whom he described as:

A true artist and a true friend.

Richter conducted the premiere in Manchester with
the Hallé Orchestra in December the same year. It
received a great critical reception and was
performed again, in London, a few days later – in
the presence of the ailing Jaeger – to a rapturous

standing ovation. In fact, at the London Symphony Orchestra rehearsal of the work, Richter issued his now famous call to arms when gathering the musicians to begin the piece, namely:

Gentlemen, let us now rehearse the greatest symphony of modern times written by the greatest modern composer – and not only in this country!

The symphony's reputation was heightened by the Manchester reviews from the previous week. Music lovers had to be turned away in droves from the second London performance.

If 1908 had ended with absolute music in the *Symphony No.1*, then 1909 and 1910 would continue with absolute passion – in the form of Alice. But this was not Alice Elgar; this was Alice Stuart-Wortley.

Initially, 1909 revealed nothing more than a continued desire for all things Italian. The Elgars holidayed in Careggi, just outside Florence, visiting Pisa, Bologna and Venice. If it was a happy holiday at first – and the beautiful *"Go, Song of Mine"*, one of Elgar's finest songs, produced in Italy in May, suggests it was – it was blackened by the news of the death of Jaeger. "Nimrod", Elgar's closest kindred spirit and musical confidant, was gone. Elgar continued his stay, and even called in on Richard Strauss, who was now living in his new

chalet in Garmisch, bought via the proceeds of his
controversial 1905 opera, *Salome*.

When Elgar Was 52 . . .

Back in the UK, Elgar received a new commission
from the London Philharmonic Society, and
immediately resurrected his initial Kreisler-driven
thoughts for a violin concerto. He stopped pretty
soon, though, not just to fit in an autumn tour
conducting with the London Symphony Orchestra,
but also to finish off some more songs. Although we
have not mentioned his songs much in this book,
Elgar's output of songs (or part-songs, as they are
often called) accounts for a huge tranche of his
output. In all he, wrote more than 50, many of
them, admittedly, to now dated words but, equally,
many of them unfairly neglected.

January 1910 saw Elgar preparing for a bitter-sweet
musical event – a memorial concert for his friend,
Jaeger. Elgar also took a London flat in order to try
to buckle down to the work on his projected *Violin
Concerto*. In February, he arranged for a private
performance of the work so far – only for violin and
piano, with the composer himself playing the piano
part. Alice Stuart-Wortley was present, as was her
husband, Charles. Charles and his wife were
immediately taken by the unfinished work. She, in
particular, was worried by Elgar's alleged musings
that he thought he might not be able to finish it.

He was, he said, having trouble finding the one theme that linked many of the separate sections together. There and then, she encouraged him to continue with his efforts, saying how distraught she would be if the work were to remain unfinished.

Fired up, that very night Elgar returned to his rented flat in Queen Anne's Mansions and set to work once again on the violin concerto. Within minutes, he had found the "missing theme" that had been eluding him. As far as Elgar was concerned, it was directly as a result of his new-found friend's encouragement. The period of influence of Alice Stuart-Wortley had begun. From this point onwards, she would be an integral part of his world.

Elgar now had the problem, though, of having two Alices in his life. Fairly early on in their extensive correspondence, therefore, he gave Alice Stuart-Wortley the nickname "Windflower", after the white flowers that were to be found in many Worcestershire woodlands. (As a result, we, too, will adopt this name for the second Alice in Elgar's life, just to avoid confusion.) Elgar also kept the date of his finding the *Violin Concerto* theme (7 February) as a personal anniversary for himself and Windflower.

By February, the nomadic composer had rented a different flat in London, this time at 38 New Cavendish Street, which was just minutes away from the Queen's Hall. Saddened by the death of King

Edward VII in May, he took the opportunity of a stay at The Hut, in Bray, to work on the *Violin Concerto*.

When Elgar Was 53 . . .

He spent much of June there, with Windflower visiting on a number of occasions during his stay. He finished the bulk of work on the first draft of the concerto and showed it to Fritz Kreisler, the violinist whose comments had inspired Elgar to start the work in the first place. Kreisler adored the work. In August, Elgar began scoring the first draft of the concerto – "our concerto", as he called it in letters to Windflower – for the full orchestra, a task that occupied him on and off until September. When it was finished, he wrote an inscription on the front page. It was a quote from novelist and playwright, Alain-René Lesage, a Frenchman who had devoted much of his life to Spanish literature. It read :

Aquí está encerrada el alma del . . . . .

It was from Lesage's 1715 work, *Gil Blas de Santillane*, and it translated as "Here is enshrined the soul of . . . . .". Enigmatic Elgar at his best again. Whose soul? He never let on. Was it Windflower, the person he credited with inspiring him to finish the piece? Was it Alice, his wife? Was it himself?

Well, as with the *Enigma Variations*, it has inspired many theories over the years, each one of them, while potentially perfectly plausible, futile. Elgar, once again, took the secret to his grave. Some commentators have flagged up the fact that the number of dots after the quotation is five, rather than the commonplace three that most would write to indicate an incomplete sentence. This, some say, means that Elgar was saying:

Here is enshrined the soul of _ _ _ _ _

That is, five blanks, one for each missing letter of the mystery dedicatee's name. If so, this would still leave us back where we started. *Alice*, his wife? *Alice* Stuart-Wortley? *Elgar* himself, even? Who knows?

Before the V*iolin Concerto*'s premiere in November, Elgar dug out some of his musical sketches from his last trip to Italy and began to start transforming them into a full orchestral work. The preparations for the *Violin Concerto*, however, were taking up most of his time. Kreisler eventually played it to an expectant public on 10 November at a concert in the Queen's Hall given by the Philharmonic Society. It went down a storm and was given a full 15 minutes of applause. (Think about that for a moment – 15 minutes of applause. Have you ever been at a concert in your life where a work was given 15 minutes of applause? Amazing!) The concerto received rave press reviews, too, and when Kreisler toured the country with the work, its fame was assured. It also received early performances in

continental Europe, courtesy of the
composer/violinist, Eugene Ysaye.

Elgar retired to Plas Gwyn for Christmas, working
on the Italian orchestral sketches. A guest for
Christmas that year was the new passion in Elgar's
life, Windflower. By January 1911, the Italian
orchestral sketches had turned into a symphony – at
least, the first movement of it. By February, though,
the first movement had three more for company
and *Symphony No. 2* was finished. Finished, in fact,
at around the same time that Elgar said "yes" to a
partnership that was to prove important in his life.
He agreed to become the Principal Conductor of
the young but influential London Symphony
Orchestra. For now, though, thoughts of the LSO
were put aside, in favour of a trip abroad.

In March, Elgar boarded the *Mauretania* for the long
voyage to the Americas. He was to tour parts of Canada
and the USA – travelling without his wife Alice, on this
occasion. Instead, he was with the Sheffield Choir on
their "Coronation" tour, one of a number of musical
events dedicated to the forthcoming crowning of
George V. Elgar was again less than enamoured of
America, though, writing back to Windflower that
even an offer of millions of dollars wouldn't be enough
to persuade him to ever settle there.

He returned to England in May and found the
country even further in the grip of coronation fever.

He himself began rehearsals of his *Symphony No. 2* at the Queen's Hall. He was in the middle of them when he heard about the death of Mahler, on 18 May. The new symphony was premiered just six days later. It gained a reserved reception. There was no 15 minutes of applause from the first-night audience and nobody said it was the greatest symphony of modern times. In hindsight, many have said that the mood of *Symphony No. 2* did not match that of a country in the grip of the excitement and optimism of a coronation and, true enough, the work did enjoy a much greater reputation after the First World War had well and truly tarnished the Edwardian golden age. Nevertheless, the premiere audience was not a full house, and numbers dwindled at each new performance.

When Elgar Was 54 . . .

Elgar embarked on his last summer at Plas Gwyn, having received a rather special birthday present. He was appointed to the Order of Merit in the coronation honours. His new march was premiered at the coronation, too, along with an anthem, *"O Hearken Thou"*, an honour that appears in no way to have made up for some of the disappointments of the reaction to the *Symphony No. 2*. Elgar was becoming depressed. He refused to attend the coronation, an amazing act made all the more amazing by his insistence that Alice didn't go, either.

It was around this time that he also broke off from his previously exclusive arrangement with his publishers, Novello. From now on, he had decided, he would sell his music to the most suitable, possibly the highest, bidder. Elgar was at a bit of a low. What was worse, though, was that he would fall lower still.

An autumn trip to Turin cheered him a little. He conducted the now world-famous *Enigma Variations,* as well as the *Introduction and Allegro for Strings.*

On New Year's Day, 1912, the new Principal Conductor of the London Symphony Orchestra moved into his new home in Hampstead, north London. Elgar christened the building "Severn House". It was a large, imposing house. Not, it has to be said, classically attractive, but it was a fitting home for the country's greatest composer. It had its own library and billiard room. Even though it was expensive to run, Elgar and Alice felt that it finally fitted the bill as a suitable home for the nation's favourite composer.

However, within days of moving in, Elgar became unwell, suffering from dizziness which led to a fall – early signs of a rather more serious problem. It wasn't helped by a quite busy work period for Elgar, either. He was in the middle of the LSO's 1911–12 season, and had also agreed to an extra job on the side – conducting something called *The Crown of India*.

Elgar had written *The Crown of India* as a commission for a piece to celebrate the Indian, colonial aspect of the king's coronation. It was well-paid, admittedly, but it was not without its problems – namely that Elgar had to conduct the first two-week run of it at the London Coliseum. (The Coliseum, incidentally, was originally a music hall and is now home to the English National Opera company.) Following a fortnight of conducting performances almost every day, Elgar found himself unwell again. At around the same time that Britain was horrified by the sinking of the *Titanic*, Elgar received the news that the noises in his ears and his continuing dizziness were caused by an illness called Ménière's Disease. His doctor ordered him to rest.

Ménière's Disease

Ménière's is a disease of the inner ear, the underlying causes of which are still unknown. When an increased volume of fluid accrues in the labyrinth, the messages sent by nerve receptors to the brain can be wrong, leading to dizziness, nausea, headaches and even hearing loss. It is not contagious or fatal but it can stay with a patient for a long time.

When Elgar Was 55 . . .

Elgar spent a month doing nothing but visiting friends. After a while, though, his desire to compose proved irresistible. Soon enough, he had unearthed the poem, "The Music Makers" by Arthur O'Shaughnessy, and began work. The importance of this piece to him, at this time in his life, is probably hard to overstate. Elgar had always felt a passionate sense of his place in society.

Despite the fact that he was, in the public's eyes at least, the country's greatest living composer, with some of his works respected around the world, he was, in his own view, still something of an outsider. He was the Catholic always knocking on the door; the tradesman's son looked down on; the self-taught, late-flowering musician and not the classic academic prodigy. These feelings, which never left Elgar, were what led him to be attracted to O'Shaughnessy, with his hymn to active, frontline music makers.

Elgar considered himself to be a man who had arrived at his place in society through active music-making, rather than through the hallowed grounds of the quad. Although O'Shaughnessy's poem is now regularly attacked for its simple, "moon–june" rhymes, there was no way it was ever going to escape the attentions of Elgar the composer, with its themes of the lonely artists who dare to dream in

order to craft their wonderful music. It was this
heady mix, combined with Elgar's frame of mind
over both his own place in society and his position
in the curve of his own career, that drove him on.
Elgar would have his new work, *The Music Makers*,
finished by July 1912.

The day after he completed it, at Severn House, he
went for a walk on Hampstead Heath and wept as
he walked, bursting with achievement over his new
work and yet, at the same time, finding the world
into which he had brought it increasingly
abhorrent. He finished the orchestrations for *The
Music Makers* by August, in plenty of time for
rehearsals for its October premiere, in Birmingham.

The Birmingham premiere of *The Music Makers* was
notable for its juxtaposition of Elgar conducting his
new work with the composer Sibelius conducting
his new *Symphony No. 4*. In the event, *The Music
Makers* was met with an opening night enthusiasm
from its audience that was not matched by the
critics, many of whom failed to understand why
Elgar was quoting some of his own pieces in the
score. Today, *The Music Makers* is recognized as a
masterpiece. It is almost a self-portrait of Elgar as
he was in 1912.

Elgar finished the year still suffering. His ears were
causing him the most worry. In its actutest form,
Ménière's Disease can lead to total deafness and,

although his was not so extreme, Elgar must have been as tormented by the thought as he was by the actual illness.

His Master's Voice

Although he was very, very fond of dogs, Elgar didn't really have much luck in keeping them. When he and Alice married, Alice refused to have his first dog in the house, so it was sent to Elgar's sister. Later, when he moved into Severn House, Hampstead, he persuaded Alice that a house near the heath was ideal for dogs and she agreed – until it decided to wet the carpets and ruin the furniture and it, too, was then sent away. A third dog ran away. Finally, after Alice's death, Elgar acquired two spaniels, Mina and Marco. As if to make up for all the time without canine friends, he would set them places at table, complete with napkins, and also telephone them when he was out. He even wrote a small orchestral piece, Mina, in honour of one of them.

The year 1913 was to see musical riots in Paris. It started, for Elgar, on holiday in Naples and Rome. This was not to be one of his extended six-month stays, though – he was busy. By March, he was back in Severn House at work on a new commission. It was for the Leeds Festival later that year and it was to be an orchestral work based on the Shakepearean character of Falstaff. Elgar was also down to be one of the festival's conductors that year, too. Although this showed some measure of how respected Elgar had become as a conductor, his conducting self-esteem received a blow in May when he found out that the London Symphony Orchestra had ended his contract. No doubt his health was a potential reason, as was the desire to name a new, big-name conductor to take over. What cannot be avoided, however, is the simple fact that the LSO's concerts under Elgar – many of which generously showcased new, up and coming composers – had not made money. Elgar was seen, by the orchestra at least, as not being the musical draw he once was.

The Opera That Never Was

You can only think it would have been something magical – an opera with music by Elgar and words by Thomas Hardy. The two were not too distant contemporaries and they happened to share the same birthday, 2 June. Elgar had often considered starting an opera, but had never found a subject that would work. He was approached, via a third party, to consider setting Hardy. Hardy wanted him to set his story A Pair of Blue Eyes, *which tells the tale of a love triangle in which a woman struggles with her feelings for an older, well-to-do man from the city and a young, more impoverished chap from the country. Elgar, however, wanted a more noble subject altogether and, alas, the partnership never happened.*

When Elgar Was 56 . . .

It was a summer of both composing and enjoying music. Elgar saw, amongst other things, Puccini's *Tosca* and Debussy's *Pelléas et Mélisande*. He also finished *Falstaff* by August.

In Leeds in October, Elgar honoured his engagement as one of the Festival's chief conductors. It must have been quite an ordeal, as a result of the enthusiastic way in which concerts were scheduled in those days. Often, promoters would think nothing of putting several very large works side by side – a number of full symphonies and concertos, back to back – meaning that a concert could occasionally start just after lunch and only finish late at night. Elgar would have had several such days as part of his contribution to the Leeds Festival that year. When it came to the premiere of his own *Falstaff*, however, he had at least had the luxury of having been out for a trip into the exquisite Yorkshire countryside to relax, beforehand. The critics could not agree on their verdict over Falstaff, even when it was played to fairly modest audiences later in London. To be fair to the critics, *Falstaff* is a hard piece to pull off in performance, with many great conductors unable to make sense of the extremely episodic nature of the score.

Thankfully for Elgar, his relationship with the record company, HMV was really prospering and he was in the studios in December to lay down versions of both *Carissima* and *Sospiri*. As the last act of 1913, *Sospiri* would provide a fitting epitaph to the golden age – a golden age that would be at an end within months.

The following year, 1914, began normally enough for Elgar, with more HMV recordings in Hayes. Indeed, this desire, this race, if you like, to record his own work only serves to highlight how mistaken are some of the cliché conceptions of Elgar. Today, he is often cast as a jingoistic, old school tie, faded symbol of old England – and yet he was, in many ways, an anti-establishment, pro-German, technophile, one of the few composers so keen to embrace the new invention of recording that he put some of his own works on record before they were premiered. He had one of the first gramophones installed in his house and one of the first telephones. He really was what the communications industry today would term "an early adopter".

When Elgar Was 57 . . .

By the time of his birthday in 1914, Elgar had not only conducted a performance of his oratorio, *The Apostles*, in Canterbury, he had also agreed to compose a third section to go alongside it – a decision he would come to regret. For now, though, the events of the next couple of months would put any thoughts of work in the shade. In July, the

Elgars, with Carice, travelled to Scotland for a
holiday. They were still there on 4 August when the
First World War was declared.

Boats, trains and cars were immediately
commandeered for troop movement and, with a
limited amount of Scottish money, Elgar was almost
confined to his Ross-shire hotel, the Gairloch.
Eventually, he made it back home, in time for the
premiere of the beautiful *Sospiri* in London. *"Land
of Hope and Glory"* was performed at the concert.
The song may well have taken on a new significance,
considering everything else that was going on in the
world. Ominously, a work by the German composer
Richard Strauss was removed from the concert. This
was a sign of the times, which would see some of
Elgar's friendships torn apart.

Elgar quickly signed up to do his bit in the war
effort, enrolling in the Special Constabulary in
Hampstead. His daughter, Carice, began work for
the Red Cross (and later the Censor's Office). "War
Fever" began to grip the nation. What had started
with a reconsideration of a Strauss piece in a concert
became a full-scale movement of reaction, with
many folk dropping any German references, not just
in concerts and the like, but even in their names.
Another English composer, Gustavus von Holst,
who was actually of Swedish descent, dropped the
"von" from his name, lest he be considered German.
In an ironic move that harked back to the *Enigma*

Variations, the widow of Elgar's friend at Novello, Jaeger, changed her name to Hunter. Many Germans, such as Elgar's friend Hans Richter, felt the need to renounce the honorary degrees that British universities had bestowed upon them.

Oddly enough, Elgar found the horrors of war in many ways an artistic spur. In December, he was moved – by the German overthrow of Belgium – to compose a work called *Carillon*, using words from a poem entitled "Après Anvers". Premiered in the strangely brewed mix of high emotions that 1914 had generated, *Carillon* was a big hit, becoming the musical talk of the nation, carried along by a huge wave of public sympathy for the plight of the Belgian people.

Elgar continued to mine his newly found seam of creative raw material, with a setting of three poems by Laurence Binyon: "For the Fallen", "To Women", and "The Fourth of August". The first of these poems, in particular, has become a perennial at Remembrance Day services, with its powerful lines:

At the going down of the sun and in the morning
We will remember them.

Despite a minor hiccup with the composer C. B. Rootham, who had already lodged an interest in setting the poem to music, Elgar's version won the day.

When Elgar Was 58 . . .

More contributions to what might be called Elgar's "war music oeuvre" came in July with the premiere of a work entitled *Polonia*. This was a show of unity with the Polish people and, hence, contained musical quotes from Chopin and Paderewski. At that time the latter was still a composer, although he would soon become Polish president when war was ended. It also included the Polish national anthem. Elgar gave all his proceeds from the premiere to the Polish Victims' Relief Fund, before leaving for a short rest break near Midhurst in Sussex.

As the war progressed throughout 1915, Elgar set to work on an escapist script by the playwright, Algernon Blackwood, called *The Starlight Express*. The story is all stardust and fairies, and perfectly demonstrates Elgar's approach to the war. On the one hand, he was right in there, pointing out the horrors, in his dedicated pieces such as *Polonia* and *Carillon*, taking the role of the artist as witness. On the other hand, he was also able to leave the horrors of war behind and to enter an escapist, child-like world.

Elgar finished this particular piece of fantasy, *The Starlight Express*, in December 1915, but missed the opening night. He stayed at home with Alice, who had been involved in a minor accident with a taxi

113

and was suffering from concussion. Her period of
enforced rest meant that Elgar stayed around the
house, engaged as full-time nurse. Some have
suggested that he wasn't sufficiently enamoured of
the production, and used his wife's problems to get
out of the opening night. Whatever the truth, he
did go along to see it later in the run.

When *The Starlight Express* ended in January, 1916,
Elgar went straight into working on a new
recording for HMV. He had been offered a brand
new contract by the record company, which would
prove extremely useful financially. Severn House
drained a lot of money in upkeep and so regular
income from HMV was a real lifeline. By March he
was back conducting his old orchestra, the LSO, on
a short tour of Scotland and the north, despite the
fact that both he and Alice were suffering from a
bout of flu. The schedule, and the flu, meant that
Elgar was soon exhausted. His Ménière's disease
flared up once again.

Nevertheless, the work didn't stop. He was in Leeds
in May for the premiere of his two (soon to be
three-) piece suite of Binyon poems, now entitled
The Spirit of England, and there were further
London performances in front of the king and
queen later. *The Spirit of England* was,
unsurprisingly, very well received, with many
critics proclaiming Elgar's poetry settings as
masterpieces.

When Elgar Was 59 . . .

Elgar took himself off to the Lake District in July for a brief holiday with both Alice and Windflower, where he became unwell with, amongst other things, a particularly sore throat. Back in London in August, he sought treatment for it and was told to have it cauterized, which he duly did. Not a pleasant process, one can imagine. Elgar found it hard to raise his spirits from this point on in 1916, and poorly attended performances of his *Symphony No. 2* did little to help. In addition, by January 1917, Elgar had heard news of the death of Hans Richter. He had actually died in early December, the previous year, but, with the constraints of war, news had not filtered through to him until January. Another of his old friends – the "Variation" G.R.S., George Robertson Sinclair – died in February, completing a spell of bad news.

Even a stunning recording of his *Violin Concerto* for HMV, featuring his ex-pupil and now renowned concert violinist, Marie Hall, was not enough to pull him out of this particular slough of despond. This may be one of the reasons, then, why Windflower took it upon herself to approach Elgar to write music for a friend's ballet. Despite still feeling unwell, Elgar agreed. The ballet was to be called *The Sanguine Fan* and Elgar began the music almost straight away. By March, *The Sanguine Fan* was ready for its premiere at London's Wyndham's

Theatre. Just a month later, Elgar had also completed the music for the third of the three poems in his *The Spirit of England*.

Elgar was still somewhat despondent. Knowing exactly what to do, Alice set out, with Carice, into the countryside to look for a place where Elgar might be able to seek refuge. She found the ideal place: Brinkwells, near Fittleworth in Sussex. Elgar adored Brinkwells, with its superb views and its woodland surroundings. Although it was a gradual process of revival, the stunning location and peaceful atmosphere would eventually have Elgar back composing furiously all day long.

When Elgar Was 60 . . .

By June, he was able to premiere his brand new "war" piece, called *The Fringes of the Fleet*, a setting of a Kipling poem, which opened at the London Coliseum. By way of research for the work, Elgar had visited the fleet itself in Harwich, where he'd been shown around as a guest of honour. Once again, Elgar found himself with a hit on his hands. This was due both to the wartime theme and the popularity of Kipling's poems. Kipling himself had originally objected to his words being used, but eventually relented.

The autumn of 1917 saw Elgar still not in his best health. He was again complaining of dizziness,

although, in October, he did manage to see the premiere of his now complete *The Spirit of England*, in Birmingham. By late November and into December, his doctors were sufficiently anxious to insist that he visit a specialist, which he did. Although nothing was discovered, Elgar continued to be under the weather well into January 1918, whereupon a fresh examination from his doctors resulted in the conclusion that he should have his tonsils removed.

After the operation, which was performed in London, Elgar returned to his Hampstead house and, the same night, scribbled down a small, mournful yet strangely lilting tune for cello, which Alice thought might make a nice string quartet. Elgar, possibly aware that it had greater, more significant potential, sent the small theme, temporarily arranged for piano, to Windflower. Little did any of them realize that the theme was to become the tune we now know and love as the main theme of the melancholic *Cello Concerto*.

Elgar convalesced at his new-found retreat, Brinkwells, and, almost immediately, the woodland house began to work its magic. He had a brief stay at The Hut in April, where the conductor Adrian Boult was also a guest, but was drawn again to Brinkwells in May. The Sussex countryside retreat was doing the trick. Elgar was back to composing from 7 am often right through until

7 pm, with breaks only for meals and long, refreshing walks.

Much of the transformation could also be put down to Elgar's feeling better; the operation had done a lot to alleviate his symptoms. Although it has often been noted that having one's tonsils removed is in no way seen as a cure for Ménière's Disease, in Elgar's case, he was instantly revived and his deafness never returned.

This spell at Brinkwells saw Elgar focussed on two things. The first was the music that was to become the *Cello Concerto*, the theme of which he had already sent and more or less dedicated to Windflower, and the second was Windflower herself. He sent her what can only be described as love letters, comparing her to the loveliest things in nature and almost aching for her to come to see him. She visited for a few days in May and then again in August.

When Elgar Was 61 . . .

Elgar had a piano delivered, too, and began composing a violin sonata almost immediately. Although the piano arrived only in August, Elgar had finished the *Violin Sonata* by September – the woodland setting of Brinkwells continuing to work its magic. Against his better judgement, he ventured to London in October, unhappy to be back in the capital. He attended the funeral of fellow composer Hubert Parry on 16 October at St Paul's Cathedral, paying his respects to a man to whom he had had a somewhat begrudging attitude in life.

On 11 of November, the day of the Armistice, Elgar went back to Brinkwells, possibly pondering a request from the poet Laurence Binyon to set some music for peace. Just as he had been initially reluctant to exhibit anti-German spirit in 1914, he now could not bring himself to write the music of peace. At least not yet. As the country was now at peace after four terrible years of war, Elgar should have had little on his mind to disturb him in the Sussex countryside. But he did. Alice had developed a cough – in fact, it had been lingering since their trip to London and it was still there. Doctors were called out in December and pronounced that Alice's lungs were fine – there was no cause for concern. Tragically, that was to prove the wrong diagnosis.

To add insult to injury, news came in mid-December that their Hampstead residence, Severn House, had been burgled. Alice journeyed up to London to sort out affairs as best she could. It was the start of what was also going to be a hard winter. The general post-war fuel shortage was also going to make the upkeep of two houses hard for the Elgars. Nevertheless, on Christmas Eve 1918, Elgar finished a string quartet, which he dedicated to the Brodksy

Quartet. It seemed only fair, since they had commissioned one from him some 20 years earlier. Better late than never. It received its first performance, in private, in January 1919, in the presence of, amongst others, George Bernard Shaw. Shaw was becoming more and more friendly with Elgar and the relationship would prove to be one which both parties cherished as time passed.

Elgar travelled again to London in March for the half-empty premiere of his *Violin Sonata* at the now defunct Aeolian Hall in New Bond Street. He stayed up in London to attend the public premiere, too, of his *String Quartet* at the Wigmore Hall in May. But taking up most of his creative time in this period was his "Windflower" piece, his "tonsillectomy" tune, if you like. This was the piece that he had started on the very night of his operation, his *Cello Concerto*. It was finished by August. It is worth pointing out, indeed, that many people refer to the *Cello Concerto* as his lament for the war. Some, – journalistic luminaries amongst them – even wrongly state that it was written upon the death of his wife. But as we see, she was alive and, if not well, then seemingly well. A far more plausible theory about the *Cello Concerto* is that, yes, it is clearly infused with a melancholy that stems at least in part from four years of horrific war, but it is also a lament for unrequited love: Elgar's love for Windflower.

"Cello, Cello, Cello . . . What's Going On 'Ere Then?"

In July 1919, two men were arrested and charged, not only for the burglary at Elgar's Severn House in Hampstead the previous December, but also for a string of other break-ins. The fact that they had been burgled by policemen led Alice to bemoan the slipping moral standards of the nation. A number of items were stolen from Elgar's house (which was unoccupied at the time), including a toast rack and many items of Elgar's clothing. Taking into account the pair's previous handiwork, the judge in their eventual trial had no hesitation in sentencing them to five years' hard labour.

When Elgar Was 62 . . .

The *Cello Concerto* was finished in August and the premiere arranged for October, as part of a London Symphony Orchestra concert. Sadly, it was to be an unsatisfactory premiere. How often have we heard those words so far in our *Friendly Guide*? Elgar's work was given scant rehearsal time because, it appears, Scriabin's 1907 work, *Poem of Ecstasy*, was harder than had been originally envisaged for the orchestra to master and, as a result, much of the time originally allotted to the *Cello Concerto* was taken up with the Russian mystic's symphonic poem. Although the soloist was superb, the orchestra was not, and Elgar was furious with Albert Coates, the conductor. At least, on this occasion,

121

the critics spotted that the orchestra was badly rehearsed. Nevertheless, it was a sad start for a now much-loved piece.

Fortunately for Elgar, following a stay in Worcester with friends, he was able to leave the country, honouring engagements to conduct in Brussels and Amsterdam, with the Concertgebouw Orchestra, leaving a now-ailing Alice at home in bed. He must have taken some cheer, at least, from the fact that, while in Belgium, he was invited to an official reception at the Ministry of Justice. There, he was publicly thanked for his contribution to the Belgian wartime morale, in his composition of his work *Carillon.*

December saw Elgar once again in the studios of HMV in Hayes to record part of his brand new *Cello Concerto* with the 28-year-old former cello prodigy, Beatrice Harrison. Although Alice's health was becoming an increasing cause for concern – she was confined to her bed when Harrison visited her in November to rehearse the piece – parts of the concerto were successfully recorded.

Elgar also began work, in January 1920, on a reworked version of his setting of Binyon's *For the Fallen* for the dedication service of Edwin Lutyens' new Cenotaph in Whitehall. This music was, in the event, not used. In February that year, in the first post-wartime show of faith in Elgar the composer, he was appointed to the council of the Royal College of Music in London.

In March, Alice was still unwell, with a seemingly permanent cough and cold. Although friends described her as frail, she was again told by doctors that there was nothing wrong. She was well enough to attend a performance of Elgar's *Symphony No. 2*, given by the London Symphony Orchestra and conducted by the 31-year-old Adrian Boult. It was a performance that seemed to re-establish the work's reputation after its originally lacklustre reception in 1911. The introspective mood of the work was much more suited to a nation that was bewildered and bloodied by war.

For Elgar, however, all thoughts of the reputation of his *Symphony No. 2* paled into insignificance when, on 26 March, he returned from a conducting engagement in Leeds to find his wife desperately unwell and in bed. Entries in his diary at the time show Elgar to be not only hugely concerned but also, perhaps, vaguely aware that his wife was not going to recover. Alice was suffering from a form of lung cancer that doctors had not been able to detect.

By April, she was in a bad way and Elgar was unable to understand her words. On the morning of 7 April, her condition was deemed to be so serious that she was given the last rites. That evening, at around 6 pm, she died in Elgar's arms.

Alice was buried at St Wulstan's Church, Little Malvern, on 10 April, 1920.

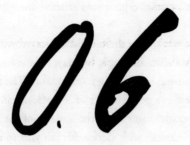

The Autumn Years

When Elgar Was 63 . . .

Elgar was nothing if not a man of many different
enigmas. Although he appeared to yearn for the
muse of *other* women in order to write his music
(most notably Windflower), nevertheless, when
Alice died, he appeared unable to compose. Alice
had dedicated the last 30 years of her life to
ensuring that her husband wrote down the music
that was in his head and, in doing so, made sure
that he yielded his maximum musical harvest
for the nation. And don't forget, this nation was
once the barren "land without music".

As a result of the combination both of her absence and of the post-war melancholy that was slowly dawning, Elgar began to experience a musical drought.

For a while after the funeral, he stayed with his sister, Pollie, although, by May, he was back honouring conducting engagements. The first of these was a performance of *The Apostles* in Newcastle. Elgar spent the remains of the summer at Brinkwells with Carice, his last visit to the place. As much as he loved it there, the landlord had decided not to extend Elgar's lease. In addition, Alice's family informed him that part of her money now reverted back to them. Elgar was said to have been angered at what he considered the last, bitter act of a family who had never fully embraced "the tradesman's son". Carice Elgar was prevented from inheriting any of her own mother's money.

One semblance of normality that did return, however, was the Three Choirs Festival, which had been cancelled during the war. Elgar's presence at this year's Worcester event was considerable. He conducted his "*For the Fallen*", as well as *The Music Makers* and *The Dream of Gerontius*. Unfortunately, for Elgar, nothing felt the same.

He visited Amsterdam and Brussels in October 1920, where he was once again honoured for his wartime contribution to the Belgian war effort. This time, King Albert of Belgium personally decorated him with the Ordre de la Couronne. He returned to England to spend Christmas with Pollie at Stoke Prior. However this, too, was to prove just another in a long line of "never agains". Pollie would move from Stoke Prior the following year and so it was Elgar's last time at a place that he loved, and where he had enjoyed so many happy times.

It is easy for us to understand why, faced with a combination of the war, the death of his wife and the modernity of the twenties (with, as Elgar himself said, its "extraordinary females"), Elgar would come to see himself as a man out of his time.

In the March of 1921, Carice became engaged to a farmer, Sam Blake, whom she had met whilst on holiday in Switzerland the previous year. Although happy for his daughter, Elgar could not seem to draw himself out of his downward spiral. One relationship, in particular, was contributing beyond all others to his melancholic state, namely that with his publisher, Novello. Elgar often felt unappreciated by Novello, even at the best of times, so when, in 1921, they paid him a mere £500 for ALL his outstanding small works and arrangements, he was nothing short of depressed: £500 for the complete remaining works of the greatest British composer of all time!

Considering that he had hardly put pen to paper since his wife had died, this was certainly not the spur Elgar needed to get him to compose. He did, in April, make

an arrangement of a Bach fugue, but as far as Elgar originals were concerned, recent sightings were scarce.

Elgar had, by now, also decided to let Severn House go, but he could not find a buyer. As a result he put the place up for auction and received not one single bid.

When Elgar Was 64 . . .

The next time you are visiting the till-beating, retail heart of London, namely Oxford Street, think of Elgar when you pass by the imposing HMV record store. Why? Because Elgar opened the original branch. At the time, Elgar was the most famous recording artist on the HMV label, recording many of his works, sometimes even before they had received their concert hall premiere, so the HMV bosses decided to ask Elgar to open the store. He cut the ribbon on 20 July, 1921. If you ever visit the store and they are blaring out Beyonce or Madonna, spare a thought for Elgar. He was there first.

A month later, and Elgar had left Brinkwells for good. By November, his Hampstead house had finally been sold at auction and Elgar had found himself a small flat at 37 St James's Place, in the heart of London. This seemingly odd decision for the man who so loved his countryside was perhaps a little more understandable when you realize that it meant that he was within walking distance of virtually every one of his London clubs.

Elgar's Clubs

Elgar was a member of a number of London clubs.

Brooks

Based in St James's Street, and originally a gaming house as well as a club. Now merged with the St James's Club.

The Savile

Named after the club's original site on Savile Row, and formerly called The New Club. It now has an Elgar Room on the third floor. Famous members included Thomas Hardy, and the motto is "Sodalitas Convivium".

The Garrick

A largely drama-based clientele, in Garrick St, London. Other famous members included Dickens, Trollope, J. M. Barrie and Millais. Motto: "The world's a stage".

The Athenaeum

Based in Pall Mall, originally a club for great thinkers, but membership widened to include all fields. Boasts winners in every category of the Nobel prize as members. Has an 80,000-title library. In an enlightened move, women were allowed to become members – in 2002.

In fact, this period appeared to show the sprouting of the first signs of renewed hope for Elgar. His central London residence afforded him the possibility of more socializing and certainly more concert going. Also, around this time, he received a new contract with HMV for recording – it was to the tune of £500 per annum (the same amount that Novello had offered him for his entire unpublished catalogue, only this was per year).

After a Christmas at Pollie's new place in Bromsgrove, Elgar busied himself for the New Year's first big event, the wedding of his daughter, Carice, to Sam Blake, which took place on 16 January. Towards the end of the month, as part of his renewed interest in the London concert scene, he attended a concert given by Richard Strauss. It was Strauss's first English engagement since the end of the war and Elgar threw a grand lunch, just a day later, inviting Strauss and a number of the then current crop of young British musicians to get together. In the end, it must have been one of those events at which any music lover would love to have been a fly on the wall. The guest list included the conductor Adrian Boult, the composers John Ireland, Arthur Bliss, Arnold Bax, Eugene Goosens and Rutland Boughton – not to mention the author George Bernard Shaw – all in the same room, with Strauss and Elgar both telling longer and longer anecdotes through interpreters.

In May, Elgar put pen to paper again – but only to complete his Bach arrangement by working on the *Fantasia* which accompanied his earlier *Fugue in C Minor*.

When Elgar Was 65 . . .

When Elgar reached 65, he was still all but retired from composition. Would the situation change? Certainly not immediately. In June, he found time to work on an orchestration of Parry's *Jerusalem*. Not many people realize that the arrangement of the work that Elgar completed that summer is the one that we almost all know and love. It is the same arrangement that has been played as a regular feature of the Last Night of the Proms every year since, seemingly, time immemorial.

One thing that occupied Elgar for much of the remainder of the year was a piano concerto. He had started it not long after the *Cello Concerto* but had never succeeded in completing it. Despite previous promises to Windflower that he would continue it – and, indeed, that it would be very much in the "Windflower" style – so far it had come to nothing. And that pattern was set to continue. It is one of the great casualties of this barren period following Alice's death. In the end, in fact, it was going to take a great war poet to bring Elgar out of his "blank-page" period.

In January 1923, Laurence Binyon approached Elgar with a request for him to set to music his play, *Arthur*. Elgar perhaps felt that the gentle commission would be just right to get himself back in the saddle. It was to be incidental music to a play: no subject to find and no words to set. As a result he said "Yes". It would be his first finished piece of music since his *Cello Concerto*. He wrote much of it while staying with Carice and by February he had finished it. The new piece was premiered in March at London's Old Vic theatre.

By April, an already partly rejuvenated Elgar moved into a new house, Napleton Grange, near Kempsey in Worcester. It was just a six-month rental but it was enough to give Elgar yet another fillip. At Napleton Grange, he completed not only arrangements of Handel and Haydn, but also the odd original song like *"The Wanderer"* and – to his own words – *"Zut! Zut! Zut!"* Well, we did say the odd original song. *"Zut! Zut Zut!"* has not since become one of Elgar's most popular works, but nevertheless, it was at least another original.

When Elgar Was 66 . . .

Later that same year, Elgar decided to take a holiday. Although it would not have been by any means the first travels without Alice, it would still no doubt have felt somewhat strange to be sightseeing and acting like a tourist without her. As if to alleviate the feeling of "things ain't what they used to be", Elgar didn't choose to go back to Italy or to Bavaria. Instead, he set off on a cruise up the Amazon, to Manaus in Brazil, a place that came complete with its own opera house. To totally shatter the image we possibly all have of Elgar, he stayed for a full two months – a thousand miles up the Amazon – arriving back in England only just in time for Christmas.

The year 1924 was to be the year of Elgar's reconnection with the Establishment part of the British music scene. He was scheduled to supervise the music for the opening of the British Empire Exhibition at Wembley, in the presence of the king. In April that year, Sir Walter Parratt died. Sir Walter had been Master of the King's Music and, upon his death, rumours began to fly that the government was planning to abolish the post. Elgar, with one eyebrow raised in indignation at the abolition of such a traditional post, the other raised in an air of potential employment, wrote to offer his services. Meanwhile, the Wembley gig served as yet another small spur to get him composing again, this time a number of songs and marches. In the end, none of them was used for the Empire Exhibition owing to a combination both of time constrictions and the king's desire for more familiar music. When the actual exhibition opened, Elgar was a little disillusioned by the ceremony's huge reliance on pomp and showmanship, rather than quality of musical offering.

Things proceeded a little more favourably in the question of what to do with the job of Master of the King's Music. Elgar's letter had, at least to some extent, served to highlight the position and make it less likely that it would be abolished. Initially, though, it was thought the 52-year-old Vaughan Williams would be given the job, as his music was, intriguingly, seen as much more English than that of Elgar. As strange a thought as that may seem to us now, Elgar was considered in some quarters to have taken on classical music in very much its European, even Teutonic form. Vaughan Williams, it was thought, had looked deep into the eyes of English music before reinterpreting it as his own. In the end, though, the folk doing the choosing decided that Elgar should be given the job, if only because he was, by then, more of a favourite with the British people than Vaughan Williams. In May, then, it was announced that Elgar would become the next Master of the King's Music, a post once held by Purcell and currently held by Sir Peter Maxwell Davies.

When Elgar Was 67 . . .

Shortly after his 67th birthday, Elgar went to Paris, to conduct both *The Dream of Gerontius* and his *Symphony No. 2.* France had never really been a heartland of Elgar lovers, with his work being appreciated much more in Germany. As a result, he was significantly encouraged when he received a standing ovation.

Sadly, the trip also led, indirectly, to his splitting from his publisher, Novello. On the surface, it was over a minor matter of something to do with the scores of *The Dream of Gerontius* but, in fact, this was just the last straw for Elgar, who had wanted to walk away from the publishers many times before.

By October, Elgar had managed to secure another lease on his previous house, Napleton Grange, and, almost as soon as he had settled back into the house, he took on the services of a secretary, a cook, a valet and a maid. He also took delivery of a brand new car – a swish, gleaming Lea-Francis F type. (Lea & Francis was a Coventry-based company which started out making bicycles before moving into motorcycles and then cars.)

The next year, 1925, saw Elgar splitting his time between his conducting engagements and simply staying home, at Napleton Grange. His recent re-engagement with his own composing led him to look again at his writing so far on the *Piano Concerto*, and, once again, it began to look as though it might one day be completed. He also took some interest in a possible third part of *The Apostles*. Some Elgar scholars have noted that a potential diminishing in his religious beliefs might, however, have eventually extinguished this idea.

When Elgar Was 68 . . .

A couple of songs did emerge from 1925, namely *"The Herald"* and *"The Prince of Sleep"*, both of them dealing with the subject of death. Sadly, Elgar's sister, Lucy, died in the October of that year at the age of 73. Elgar wrote in his letters that his dog, Marco, was the only thing left to him now. A Gold Medal from the Royal Philharmonic Society cheered him only temporarily as the year ended with an operation for haemorrhoids.

The year 1926 continued very much in the sporadic, fitful vein as had 1925. Compositionally, the year was completely barren. Elgar did continue his fruitful relationship with HMV, laying down recordings of the *Enigma Variations*, the *Cockaigne Overture* and the *Pomp and Circumstance Marches Nos.1 and 2*, as well as other works. It was a useful musical outlet for Elgar at a time when he felt that he couldn't contribute to his compositional oeuvre.

In April, that year, Charles Stuart-Wortley, husband of Windflower, died. After the funeral, Windflower herself immediately travelled to Switzerland for a long holiday. She was away for five months.

When Elgar Was 69 . . .

The latter half of the year brought forth no new compositions. Elgar did conduct his *Violin Concerto*

in November; he did see Windflower for the first time since her husband's death, but his main concern seems to have been a preoccupation with his own ennoblement. Elgar valued highly the recognizable trappings of success. His push to become the Master of the King's Music, for example, was perhaps more to do with a desire for acknowledgement than any great sense of musical devotion to the king. So it was that, during the latter half of 1926, the idea of some sort of honour seemed to occupy him – so much so that he wrote to Windflower on the subject, who said she would ask questions on his behalf. Elgar, perhaps somewhat immodestly, thought there was scope for his forthcoming seventieth birthday to be used as the excuse for such an honour.

In the February of 1927, he continued his amazing series of recordings with HMV, taping a version of *The Dream of Gerontius*, something he followed up with both *The Music Makers* and *Symphony No. 2*. In April, he also recorded versions of his *Pomp and Circumstance Marches Nos. 3 and 4*. For posterity, HMV also taped one of the rehearsals, so leaving us a unique record of Elgar the conductor at work, not to mention a chance to hear what Elgar's voice sounded like.

When Elgar Was 70 . . .

To celebrate his 70th birthday, Elgar conducted a programme, made up entirely of his own music, with the BBC Wireless Orchestra, although he must have been disappointed that the venue, the Queen's Hall, was only half full. At the end of the evening, which was being broadcast, Elgar spoke the closing words, "Good night, everybody! Good night, Marco!" In case it's slipped your mind, Marco was his pet spaniel.

It was also around this time that he celebrated his birthday with a private concert of chamber music at the The Hut. By now, though, The Hut was owned by a New Zealand couple, The Wyldes, who had renamed the place "The Long White Cloud" (the early Polynesian name for New Zealand itself). Frank Schuster himself was still around, but Elgar felt that The Hut was not the same, that the whole atmosphere had changed. The chamber concert was also attended by the new, fashionable young things – people like William Walton who would have been just 25, and members of the Sitwell clan. For Elgar, nothing was quite as it should have been.

When, in December the same year, Frank Schuster died, Elgar's wistful, melancholic feelings were complete. Schuster left Elgar £7,000 in his will. To put that into some sort of perspective, the sale of the huge Severn House in Hampstead had realized only £6,500. Schuster explained in his will that he was leaving Elgar the money as a thank you for saving English music and for "being an English

composer worthy to rank with the great masters".
Christmas must have been a bitter-sweet time for
Elgar, aged 70.

In the New Year Honours list for 1928, Elgar was
made a Knight Commander of the Royal Victorian
Order. It is the second highest rank of the British
order of knighthood, and only in the personal gift
of the monarch himself. Elgar was disappointed that
he had not received a peerage.

In the spring of 1928, Elgar moved house yet again,
this time to the white Georgian splendour of
Tiddington House, near Stratford-upon-Avon.
Perhaps, with his recent bequest, and his ongoing
earnings from both conducting and HMV, he felt
he could now afford it. It was a very grand place,
with stables, courtyard, an ample garage for his
Lea-Francis car, and a boathouse. Elgar enjoyed
making good use of the large river frontage for
fishing.

George Bernard Shaw, who was by now Elgar's firm
friend, was a frequent visitor to Tiddington House
and it is said that he and Elgar would each occupy
an end of the dining room's long, wooden table,
while eating their dinners with napkins tucked into
their collars.

When Elgar Was 71 . . .

It was here in Tiddington House that Elgar wrote his first new music in quite some time – and again, it was incidental music to a play that tempted him. The Birmingham Theatre Royal was to stage a production of Bertram Matthews' play, *Beau Brummel*, in November. Elgar agreed not only to supply original music, but also to be in the pit to conduct the orchestra. The rest of the year played itself out in a somewhat subdued, yet hopeful manner. He penned a Christmas carol, *"I Sing the Birth"*, in October and a fresh recording of his *Cello Concerto* was made with Beatrice Harrison. HMV had now moved up to the new "electronic" method of recording and were keen to put down new versions of pieces they had recorded via the old method. Surviving from later this year are recordings, too, of Elgar "improvising" in a compositional/classical manner – priceless recordings, made with just a rudimentary tape recorder, which show Elgar using the piano in a free-form way as a precursor to composition.

January 1929 saw the UK in the grip of one the severest winters of the 20th century and, for Elgar, it marked a personal low point, too. He conducted a concert of *The Dream of Gerontius* with the Hallé Orchestra in Manchester, only to suffer the ignominy of significant numbers of people leaving long before the end. A stream of people passed along the edge of the stage where Elgar was conducting, in order to get to the door. Elgar was, not surprisingly, utterly disillusioned. For him, it was confirmation of what he had been thinking and indeed saying for some time – that he was out of his time, and that the British people no longer appreciated his music.

When Elgar Was 72 . . .

Just a few weeks after his 72nd birthday, Elgar was out on a drive with his chauffeur, Richard Mountford. While driving, he's said to have suddenly shouted for Mountford to stop the car, whereupon he asked for manuscript paper. As none could be found – and as they were miles from anywhere – Elgar was handed an Ordnance Survey map of the Gloucester and Cheltenham area. Instantly, he began scribbling on the only blank space, the back cover of the map. He quickly sketched out three large staves and began to write down a tune that had just popped into his head. It took him just moments, with Mountford looking on from the front seat, anxiously. It was actually a version of a tune he had written much earlier, when he was the music director of the Powick Asylum, but, at this point, he had had a flash of inspiration as to how he could put it to good use. Soon afterwards, he worked on the tune at home and it became none other than the brand new *Pomp and Circumstance March No. 5*.

When the Three Choirs Festival came around in the late summer, Elgar rented yet another new house – but this time, it was to be his last. It was called Marl Bank, in Worcester, and its lofty, position on the eastern side of the city afforded Elgar a sweeping view of the cathedral. At first he rented it, just for the festival, but then, in December, he walked across the threshold as its new owner.

Call Me

A moment of trivia, here. When Elgar moved into his new house, Marl Bank, he immediately had a telephone put in. His telephone number was Worcester 924, and his telegraphic address was, simply, "Elgar, Worcester".

By 1930, the annual Crystal Palace Brass Band Competition had become something of a fixture on the musical calendar, having already been going some 24 years. For its 25th anniversary year, the organizers decided to do not just themselves but British music a favour by commissioning Elgar to come up with a new work. Elgar accepted the commission – again, perhaps, the non-orchestral, seemingly small-scale nature of the work meant it was not as daunting a prospect as a new symphony, for example. His friend George Bernard Shaw had been badgering him for some time to "cap it all" with another symphony, in fact, and it may be that Elgar had already started on some initial jottings.

Elgar was also to work with an "arranger" on the project, who would better know the technical demands of the brass instruments. He soon looked to his old music notebooks for old tunes that might be reworked for the new project and, before long, a collection of older sketches and new ideas became *The Severn Suite*. Sadly, the brass arrangement, by one Hubert Geehl, proved controversial in so far as Geehl rejected many of Elgar's ideas on how to orchestrate the brass. As a result, Elgar, dissatisfied with the resulting brass version, eventually went on to rescore the suite for orchestra – a medium of which he was a master.

Elgar's Viola Concerto

No, don't worry. There isn't really an entire concerto that you knew nothing about. But there is an Elgar Viola Concerto. In March, 1930, Elgar went back to the score of his Cello Concerto and thought it would be a good idea to rework it – for viola. Some of the tunes had to be rephrased to fit in with the difference in registers but, on the whole, Elgar was pleased with it. If you hadn't heard about it, then don't be surprised – it's not performed very often and the first recording was not made until 1989.

In May, Elgar dispatched his finished *Pomp and Circumstance March No. 5* – the one started on the back of an Ordnance Survey map – to the publishers, Boosey & Hawkes. He was insulted to receive an offer of just £75. There was good news, though, on the publishing front around this time; it came from the firm Keith Prowse. They offered Elgar a good retainer for just three songs per year, and Elgar signed up.

When Elgar Was 73 . . .

Although Elgar had been suffering from sciatica throughout the summer of 1930, he was cheered, as was the country as a whole, at the news that the Duchess of York had given birth to a baby daughter, Margaret Rose (Princess Margaret) in August. Bonfires were lit at her birthplace, Glamis Castle in Scotland. Together with her four-year-old sister, Elizabeth Alexandra Mary (Queen Elizabeth), who had only recently appeared on the cover of *Time* magazine, the royal children proved to be the new inspiration that Elgar needed. After the premiere of his *Severn Suite* at the Crystal Palace Brass Band Championships in September – with its dedicatee, George Bernard Shaw, in attendance – Elgar began to look again to his old notebooks for a suitable response from the Master of the King's Music to the birth of the new princess. He worked up some of his jottings into one of his loveliest works to date, *The Nursery Suite*.

The new piece received its private premiere, in two sittings, at HMV's Kingsway Hall studios in London, with the Duke and Duchess of York (later to be George VI and Queen Elizabeth) in attendance. By all accounts, the royal party loved the work so much, they requested encores.

Sadly, Elgar's renewed composing confidence was undermined by the furore surrounding the comments of the Cambridge music professor, E. J. Dent. In an obscure German music tome, Dent wrote that Elgar's music was:

. . . too emotional and not quite free from vulgarity . . .

. . . arguing that it was inferior to that of Parry and Stanford.

Naturally, Elgar was wounded and soon the national newspapers filled up with letters of indignation at Dent's attack. One letter, indeed, was signed by a bevy of Elgar's supporters – no fewer than 18 signatories in all – including Philip Heseltine (aka the composer Warlock) William Walton, the artist Augustus John and, of course, George Bernard Shaw.

When Elgar Was 74 . . .

When the King's Birthday Honours were announced in June, Elgar was awarded a baronetcy, a promotion, as it were, on his KCVO, making him First Baronet of Broadheath. It was a timely award and must have helped Elgar's confidence, as did, no doubt, the

October performance of his *Symphony No. 2* in London. Not only was the concert hall full to the rafters, but the applause for Elgar was overwhelming.

Interestingly enough, in the audience at that concert was a 16-year-old Benjamin Britten, and, far from exulting in the applause for Elgar, he hated the evening. It was dreadful, he said – he was so bored, he left before it had ended.

In November, Elgar was invited to open HMV's brand new recording studios in St John's Wood, the now famous Abbey Road studios. The first recording in the studios was Elgar's *Falstaff*.

John, Paul, George, Ringo and Eddie

Abbey Road is probably the best known recording studio in the world, and perhaps the only one that has crossed over from the recording industry world into the national consciousness to become a household name. This came about largely as a result of its association with the Beatles, and their landmark, eponymous album cover, showing the Fab Four walking barefoot across the nearby zebra crossing. But did you know that, when Abbey Road studios opened in 1931, the first recording ever made there was Elgar's Falstaff, *with the composer himself conducting? He only had three years left to live at the time and recorded with the London Symphony Orchestra on the very day the studio opened for business.*

November was also a big month for Elgar for other reasons. He attended a rehearsal of the Croydon Philharmonic Orchestra. It was an orchestra that Elgar had agreed to rehearse because of its close connections with his good friend, William Reed, the leader of the London Symphony Orchestra. In the front row of the fiddle players was a woman by the name of Vera Hockman. She had caught Elgar's eye during the session and Elgar clearly felt there was enough of a spark to approach her afterwards. He then suggested that they might meet at a later date, which they did.

Had Elgar found a new muse?

The two met up at the Langham Hotel, one of Elgar's regular London haunts and very much a popular place with the rich and famous of the day; Noel Coward was a regular. Elgar then invited Vera to Worcester. The relationship appeared to blossom and Vera reciprocated with an invitation to her aunt's. She also met some of Elgar's friends, although not, it should be said, Windflower. It is said that Elgar addressed her as his "sweetest and dearest". She also became a friend to Carice, with whose age she was more in line (Carice was 41, while Vera was in her thirties. Elgar, of course, was 74). It appeared to give Elgar a renewed enthusiasm for his work, and he entered into a plan to write a new *Falstaff* overture for the opening of the Shakespeare Memorial Theatre and also worked on the orchestration of the *Severn Suite*. In no way could this be called a rebirth of his creativity. At the same time, somewhat incongruously, despite Elgar having chauffeurs, maids, valets and, indeed, living in some style, he nevertheless needed a loan of £1,000 from George Bernard Shaw.

In February 1932, Elgar was shown the plans for the design of the Shakespeare Memorial Theatre, completed by Elizabeth Scott. His reaction was to exclaim that it was one of the ugliest buildings he had ever seen. He instantly withdrew from the project.

When Elgar Was 75 . . .

July brought better news. Elgar had, for many years, been hoping that the violinist and composer Fritz Kreisler would record his *Violin Concerto*. After all, it was Kreisler who had inspired its composition more than 20 years earlier. Despite the fact that Kreisler had continued to play the concerto, he refused to be pinned down to a recording of it. As a result, at HMV's suggestion, a 16-year-old "Wunder"-fiddler by the name of Yehudi Menuhin was approached, and a date set aside in July for a recording at Abbey Road's Studio 1. This is the sister to the more famous Studio 2, which has been home to not only all the Beatles recordings, but also to legendary rock albums such as Pink Floyd's *Dark Side of the Moon* and iconic film scores such as John Williams's *Star Wars*.

Elgar was delighted with Menuhin's recording of his *Violin Concerto*, referring to him as the "wonderful boy". He was so proud that he even held a playback session using his own gramophone player. Among the guests were George Bernard Shaw and T. E. Lawrence, who is better known as "Lawrence of Arabia".

Yehudi Menuhin played the *Violin Concerto* with the London Symphony Orchestra at the Royal Albert Hall later that year. Then, almost out of the blue, in December 1932, with the sound of "Elgar's 75th Birthday " concerts still ringing in the nation's ears, Elgar was approached by Sir John Reith and commissioned to write a third symphony. Reith had, in fact, been lobbied by George Bernard Shaw, who had previously encouraged Elgar to "cap it all" with a third symphony, and was well aware of Elgar's still precarious finances. Elgar accepted the commission and, indeed, began to commit some initial sketches to paper. Ominously, though, he appended a short line to one particular page of notes:

Will never be finished.

Nevertheless, by February 1933, some of the initial sketches were being completed. At the same time, there was bad news coming out of Germany. Adolf Hitler had been made Chancellor in January and, with the burning of the Reichstag at the end of

February, his powers had been increased to "police state" levels. Awful and depressing news began to seep out of Germany, which left Elgar dispirited. In April, he told Reith that his symphony would not be ready, as agreed, for October 1933 but only for May 1934. Then, on 25 April, Elgar had a seizure.

Carice, who had been visiting her father at Marl Bank at the time, was forced to call the doctors no fewer than three times in one evening. Just days later, Elgar wrote his last letter to Windflower. He made no mention of his seizure. However, he was sufficiently recovered, by May, to take his first aeroplane flight, from Croydon Airport to Paris, where he was to conduct the *Violin Concerto* with Yehudi Menuhin performing, in the presence of the French President, Gaston Doumergue.

Fascinatingly, Elgar took time out, after the concert, to visit another great English composer, Frederick Delius, at his house in Grez-sur-Loing, where it's said they sat outside Delius's home, sipping champagne and talking about music and the arts.

When Elgar Was 76 . . .

The Birthday Honours brought yet more decorations dropping onto Elgar's welcome mat at Marl Bank. This time, it was a GCVO – Knight Grand Cross of the Royal Victorian Order. In a seemingly discourteous display of indifference, Elgar did not attend his investiture.

To be fair to him, he was, by this time, not feeling anywhere near 100%. When he conducted a Prom performance of his *Second Symphony* in August, he did so seated in a chair on the podium, and several onlookers noted how he had lost weight and that his conducting suffered because of his very shaky hands. Nevertheless, he was able to conduct a recording of his *Serenade for Strings*, back at Kingsway Hall, as part of his contract with HMV.

In September, Elgar experienced what he thought was pain from recurring sciatica. In October, he went into a nursing home in Worcester for an operation and this revealed that he was, in fact suffering from inoperable cancer. His condition soon became grave enough for him to be given the last rites. It was around this time that William Reed visited him. Elgar, aware that he had yet to finish his *Symphony No. 3* and now had little time to do so, specifically told Reed not to let anyone tinker with it, should he die.

By January, 1934, Elgar had returned home to Marl Bank, complete with a supply of morphine and a nurse from the Worcester nursing home to look after him. Although weak and confined to his bed, he was nevertheless able to supervise a recording session of extracts from his *Caractacus*, by phone, thanks to a specially installed speaker relay system from Abbey Road. The session cheered Elgar enormously, yet also took a lot out of him.

By February, he was seriously ill. He is said to have often heard music playing in his room when it was silent. He did, however, refuse to see a priest, having only recently commented to a friend that he thought there was no afterlife, only oblivion. Eventually, though, last rites were administered – by a Jesuit priest, Fr Gibb, from St George's. Throughout this time, Windflower could not visit him as she was, herself, too unwell to travel.

With only his nurse by his side, Elgar died in the early hours of 23 February. "He just died," she said, "he didn't say anything."

He was 76.

Elgar was buried next to his wife, Alice, at St Wulstan's, Little Malvern.

Windflower died on 1 January, 1936.

Carice died on 16 July, 1970.

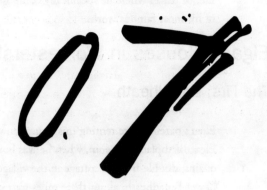

An Elgar Map
of Britain

How many houses do you expect to inhabit in your
lifetime? Some wonderfully lucky people stay in the
same place their entire life, so escaping the dubious
joys of estate agents and tea chests. Elgar was *not*
such a person. In fact, the number of houses Elgar
lived in – not all of them were homes – reached
into the twenties. If you add in the places he and
his wife rented as second homes, you get nearer 30.
Add a third layer of the homes of friends, where he
spent summers, or long holidays, and you start to
wonder if Elgar didn't have some nomadic blood in
him, somewhere along the line. We haven't itemized
them all here. Instead, we've decided to highlight

only the main homes that were important in his life, or places where he specifically composed some of his most famous works.

Elgar's Houses in Worcestershire

The Firs, Broadheath

Elgar's parents were renting this house, now the Elgar Birthplace Museum, when he was born. It's a quaint, double-fronted cottage in the village of Lower Broadheath, about three miles west of Worcester. Although it was only his home for a couple of years, Elgar always had a particular affinity with it – perhaps because it looked like the sort of house a composer should have been born in. Take the A44 out of Worcester town centre, then take a left onto Crown East Lane. The Birthplace Museum is on your right, close to the Plough Inn (where there is a fair-sized beer garden, and where children are allowed in the restaurant). The house still comprises six rooms on two floors, much as it did in Elgar's day, but it now boasts an impressive visitor and research centre across the way, committed to spreading the Elgar word.

1 Edgar Street (now Severn Street) Worcester

Elgar lived in what is now Severn Street between the ages of two and four. The larger house was

necessary to accommodate the Elgars' burgeoning
family, but it was much less to the liking of Elgar's
mother, Ann, than the country setting of The Firs.
Severn Street is just a few hundred yards from
Worcestershire County Cricket Ground, and a
stone's throw, as the name now suggests, from the
River Severn. The Worcester Porcelain Museum is
on the same street – worth a visit for enthusiasts.

2 College Precincts, Worcester

Another one of Elgar's old haunts that still stands
today, on a delightful cobbled precinct right next to
Worcester Cathedral. This was to be the family
home for just two years before a further move. In
fact, Elgar's mother and father had lived here before.
That time, Elgar's brothers and sisters, Harry, Pollie
and Lucy were born here. If you want somewhere to
stay, Burgage House Bed and Breakfast is literally
next door at 4 College Precincts, so you can sample
Worcester life from almost the same vantage point
as the man himself.

10 High Street, Worcester

The family moved into the three floors above Elgar's
father's music shop in 1863, when Elgar was just six
years old. Elgar stayed for what was, for him, quite
a long time – 16 years – the longest time he spent
at any one house throughout his life. As a result, it
would have been from this house, past which the

trams ran, that most of Elgar's formative memories sprang, when he was aged between six and 22. The house was also, of course, a direct physical influence on the young composer, since his father's music shop was directly under it and he absorbed the musical atmosphere from day to day. He would often borrow scores or improvise on instruments. It was a four-storey terraced shop, with a classic square bay window, and a sign above the first floor that read, "Elgar Brothers". Elgar's father, William, had invited Elgar's uncle, Henry, to join him. Sadly, the shop is no longer standing.

It would have been while at 10 High Street, that Elgar wrote the youthful music for a family play, presented by himself and his brothers and sisters for the pleasure of their parents. Elgar – fastidious keeper of a compositional notebook – kept the music and reworked it later as his suite, *The Wand of Youth*. He also wrote his first song, *"The Language of Flowers"*, here, as well as settings of both *Salve Regina* and *Tantum Ergo*. During his time here, he also left school and dabbled briefly with the legal profession, before realizing that his career path lay in music.

Loretta Villa, 35 Chestnut Walk (now 12 Chestnut Walk)

When Elgar was 22, he moved out of the family home above the shop in Worcester High Street. He

moved in with his newly married elder sister, Pollie
– a common practice for young men at the time.
The house is now called 12 Chestnut Walk and is
just a little less central, towards the Rainbow Hill
part of the town, not far from Worcester Foregate
Station, and still only minutes from where he had
been living. Elgar stayed here for four years, during
which time he began writing for his own wind
quintet, made up of himself, some friends and his
brother Frank – music he called his "shed music", as
they all rehearsed in the shed behind his father's
music shop. It was while here that he also managed
to visit Paris to hear Saint-Saëns, and to visit
Leipzig, to hear the music of Wagner and
Schumann. He also swelled the ranks of violins by
one, in a Birmingham concert orchestra. Other
musical associations with this house? Well, Elgar
moved in at the same time that he took on a new
job, which earned him £30 a year, as Music
Director of the Worcestershire County Lunatic
Asylum, based at Powick. Pollie's house is still there
– now numbered 12, not 35.

Forli, Alexandra Road, Malvern Link

After a short foray into the musical world of
London, Elgar decided he would be better off,
financially, if he returned to Worcestershire. So, in
1891, he moved into a semi-detached house in
Malvern Link, an area just to the northeast of Great
Malvern and separated from it by Malvern Link

Common. Despite the fact that Forli was not ideal for Elgar – it had no views over his much loved Malvern Hills – he managed to write some of his most beautiful and enduring works here, namely the *Serenade for Strings*, the *Chanson de Matin* and *Chanson de Nuit* and even the *Enigma Variations*. Other Forli works include the cantatas *The Black Knight*, *King Olaf* and most of *Caractacus*, as well as the oratorio *The Light of Life* (*Lux Christi*).

Forli is a surprising house for a blossoming composer. When you first come across it, you think that its occupant was more likely to have been a Reggie Perrin than a Great British Composer. It was semi-detached, too, which seems odd. Were Elgar's neighbours happy about the music?

Incidentally, Elgar isn't the only local Malvern Link hero celebrating a special anniversary around now: 2007 is the 150th anniversary of Elgar's birth. The Morgan Motor Company, just two minutes round the corner in Pickersleigh Road, and makers of a fittingly British sports car, is celebrating its centenary in 2009. Other local heroes include the Perrins of Lea & Perrins, makers of the internationally renowned Worcestershire Sauce. Dyson Perrins School, in Malvern Link, is named after Charles William Dyson Perrins, one-time owner of Lea & Perrins, and benefactor and eventual owner of the Royal Worcester Porcelain Factory.

Craeg Lea, Wells Road, Great Malvern

Craeg Lea is a large, detached house, imposingly set about a mile out of Malvern centre, heading south along Wells Road. The name reflects Elgar's lifelong love of wordplay: Craeg Lea is an anagram of A & E & C Elgar (the C being for his daughter Carice). From his composing room on the first floor, Elgar could see across the beautiful Severn valley, with the gentle hills rising in the distance. "I get a wonderful view of the surrounding country," he wrote. The view clearly worked to great effect as he was able to write the *Cockaigne Overture*, *In the South* and the *Pomp and Circumstance Marches Nos. 1 and 2* while sitting in front of this first-floor window. Wells Road takes its name from the then recently formed Malvern Wells village (originally part of South Malvern), which in turn takes its name from the area's famous water cures. If you're visiting in September, you might witness the Well Dressing Competition, in which the many different fountains and wells are decorated and judged. Previous winners include the West Malvern Tap (2005) and the Earl Beauchamp Fountain (2004).

Napleton Grange, Kempsey

Elgar was living here when he was made Master of the King's Music in 1924. Fittingly, it is a timbered affair, a fine and stately mansion, suited to a country gent. By now, Elgar was on his own: Alice

died in 1920. Kempsey is about three miles south of
Worcester, close to the M5, and less than half a mile
from the River Severn. Musically, it was quite a slow
period for Elgar, with the *Empire March* and the
lesser known incidental music for *King Arthur*
topping the list. Elgar took to visiting the races
regularly and even looking up old haunts of his
youth. If you're in the area, The Anchor Inn on the
Main Road serves a nice Old Speckled Hen.

Marl Bank, Rainbow Hill, Worcester

Elgar's last home, purchased in 1929 and now,
sadly, demolished. To a widower, it must have been
an enormous place, with its six bedrooms, many
reception rooms and sprawling gardens. Marl Bank
was in the eastern Rainbow Hill area of Worcester,
with commanding views of the cathedral. Musically,
these autumn years in Worcester proved to be
fruitful: The *Severn Suite*, *Pomp and Circumstance
March No. 5*, the *Nursery Suite*, as well as work on
the unfinished *Symphony No. 3*.

Elgar's House in Hereford

Plas Gwyn, Hampton Park Road, Hereford

Elgar lived in Plas Gwyn from 1904 to 1912. It is
an impressive house, set in its own secluded
grounds on the eastern outskirts of Hereford. While
Elgar was resident, it had bright, striped awnings

covering the windows, which seemed to somehow lend it an Italianate air.

Musically, this was a great time: *Pomp and Circumstance March No. 3*; the amazing *Introduction and Allegro for Strings*; the *Violin Concerto*; two symphonies; and of course, *The Music Makers*, his self-quoting cantata, parts of which he is said to have written while fishing in the River Lugg, near Mordiford Bridge, only a short bicycle ride from Plas Gwyn. This was also the place where Elgar built himself "The Ark", a converted outhouse, which he fashioned into a homemade chemical laboratory.

Elgar's Houses in London

51 Avonmore Road, West Kensington

Although he was not here long, there is a plaque to commemorate his stay. *Froissart* was composed here.

Severn House, 42 Netherhall Gardens, Hampstead

Sadly, Severn House is now long since demolished, but Netherhall Gardens is still very much in existence. It was here that Elgar finally thought he had a house fit for a Great British composer – complete with his own library.

58 New Cavendish Street

Not far from Oxford Circus and, again, another very short stay. Long enough, though, for Elgar to compose part of the *Violin Concerto* here.

as well as. . .

St James's Place, W1

3 Marloes Road, West Kensington

Oaklands, Fountain Road (now Drive), Upper Norwood

Places Elgar Rented for a While

Birchwood Lodge, Great Storridge (Worcestershire)

One of Elgar's summer houses. He wrote *Sea Pictures* here and parts of *The Dream of Gerontius*. There's a lovely photograph of Elgar and Alice, standing outside Birchwood, posing. Elgar has his arms folded and, with his trademark downward-looming handlebar moustache, he somehow has the appearance of an impatient father. You can almost hear him barking to the photographer: "Oh, come on, get on with it." Alice is looking on, demurely.

Brinkwells, Fittleworth, Sussex

One of Elgar's favourite places, where he really felt he could get away from it all. The house is not far from Bedham, and it was here that he wrote the *Cello Concerto*, the *Violin Sonata* and various chamber works.

Friends' Homes

The Hut, Bray, Berkshire (The Long White Cloud)

The Hut was owned by Elgar's friend Frank Schuster and it was usually a summer place for the composer. If you have been lucky enough to have visited Heston Blumenthal's amazing restaurant in Bray, The Fat Duck, then you have been within spitting distance of The Hut. The hut is on the Thames at Monkey Island, now home to the Monkey Island Hotel, an idyllic place where summer tea on the lawn, watching the launches pootling by, has never felt so good. The hotel is also very popular for upmarket wedding receptions, with brides and grooms having their snaps taken in sight of one of Elgar's favourite holiday homes, where he wrote much of the music to his *Violin Concerto*. It was renamed The Long White Cloud – in Elgar's day – when it was bought by a New Zealand couple, and bears that name to this day. If you ever visit Monkey Island for tea and cucumber sandwiches, try to blot out the motorway in the distance – which obviously would never have troubled Elgar – and think, instead, of that magical impromptu concert of Elgar's chamber music in 1927. Apart from Elgar and Schuster, a young William Walton was in attendance, as were members of the Sitwell clan. There was also one evening in 1904 when both Elgar and Richard Strauss came for dinner with Schuster here. Schuster left Elgar a large amount of money in his will, not only because of their friendship – Elgar called him "the most loving, strongest and wisest friend man ever had" – but also for having done so much for English music.

Jaeger's house: 37 Curzon Road, Muswell Hill

The home of Elgar's great champion – and one of his fondest friends – now bears a plaque. He was only here for a few years (1902–1909), but Elgar visited him regularly.

Pollie's house: The Elms, near Stoke Works, Stoke Prior (near Bromsgrove)

Elgar was a frequent visitor to his sister Pollie's, considering it a haven, a place of refuge.

Dr Charles Buck's house: Market Place, Settle (now a NatWest bank)

It was here that Elgar supposedly wrote his *Salut d'Amour* in the summer of 1888. Dr Buck left here in 1906.

Elgar's honeymoon: Ventnor, Isle of Wight

Elgar stayed in Alexandra Gardens for his honeymoon in 1889. There is a plaque on the house he rented.

Have a Listen Yourself. Part 1: The *Enigma Variations*

Elgar and the Enigma

Elgar's *Enigma Variations* is one of the best loved pieces of classical music in the repertoire. It became more or less an instant hit following its first performance and remains so today. How, though, was it born? What was Elgar doing and thinking when he wrote it? And, of course, what is the "enigma"? Well, we'll come to that later, but first, here is the diary of what was written when.

The Making of a Masterpiece

It is October, 1898 and Elgar is 31. He is not yet a nationally and internationally renowned composer but he does have some hefty works under his belt. For the thriving festival scene, he has already written the cantatas *King Olaf* and *The Black Knight* and the oratorio *The Light of Life* (*Lux Christi*). In addition, he has already penned both the *Salut d'Amour* for violin and piano, when he was just 22, and the masterly *Serenade for Strings* four years later. As well as all this, the first half of 1898 saw Elgar hard at work on his latest cantata, *Caractacus*, the first performance of which had only just take place, on 5 October, at the Leeds Festival, to mixed reviews. By late October, a frustrated Elgar had written to his publisher:

. . . if I write a tune, you all say it's commonplace – if I don't, you all say it's rot . . .

That letter was dated 20 October.

The next day, Elgar was back giving violin lessons at The Mount School in Malvern. He returned home that evening, for dinner with his wife, Alice. Afterwards, he lit a cigar and retired to the piano, where he amused himself improvising and playing various tunes that were in his head. At one point, one of the tunes caught Alice's ear and she asked him what it was. He told her it was just a tune he had been tinkering with, at which point she told him she liked it. Elgar then went on to describe how some of his friends might have played the tune, based on their characters. Elgar's friend, Hew Steuart-Powell, a pianist, might have played it like this, he said. Or his friend, Basil Nevinson, a cellist, might have played it like this; and William Baker, a friend of Alice's, might have played it this way. Both Alice and Elgar were amused and cheered by the three variations on Elgar's theme, no doubt firing the composer's imagination.

By 24 October, Elgar had sketched another version of the tune for his friend at Novello, the publisher, August Jaeger. At this point, though, the variations came to a temporary halt, and Elgar wrote to Jaeger on 11 November that work on them was slow.

On 5 February 1899 though, Elgar began work on the full score of the variations, something that took him just two weeks – it was finished by 19 February.

Two days later, on 21 February, Elgar sent the finished score, via a third party, to the conductor, Hans Richter, with a view to his agreeing to conduct the premiere of the work. By 24 March, Elgar had word back that Richter had agreed to conduct the premiere, at a concert on 19 June.

Elgar then worked on a piano reduction of the full score, which was complete by the end of March. He sent this, and the returned full score from Richter, to his publishers, Novello, on 8 April. Somewhere around this period – late March, early April – Elgar asked Jaeger, his contact at Novello and close friend, to add the word "enigma" above the main tune. To remind you, that was the tune he had played to Alice at the piano the previous October.

On 10 April, Elgar was approached in writing by one A. C. Barry, who had been commissioned to pen the programme notes for the concert at which the variations would be premiered. It was in his reply that Elgar first talks about exactly what the "enigma" is. Or, should we say, what the "enigmas" are. Elgar wrote:

The Enigma I will not explain – its dark saying must be left unguessed . . . Further, through and over the whole set, another and larger theme "goes", but is not played . . .

On 3 June, the members of the Hallé Orchestra arrived at the old St James's Hall, in London's Piccadilly, for the first rehearsal of the work. A second took place on 17 June, followed by a morning rehearsal on 19 June. That evening, Hans Richter conducted the Hallé Orchestra in the world premiere – which was a triumph.

Elgar's *Variations on an Original Theme* – or, as it is almost universally known, *The Enigma Variations* – was born.

"To My Friends Pictured Within"

Elgar's *Enigma Variations* consists of 15 movements. The first is the main tune, which is followed by 14 different variations on that tune. In some cases, the way in which the tune is varied is immediately discernible; in others, the connection to the original theme is negligible – such as in the 10th variation, which uses an old tune Elgar had written over 10 years earlier and originally intended for another work.

Each variation comes with a written reference to a friend of Elgar's or Alice's, either in the form of initials, or in the form of a name. In almost every case, the person hidden in the variation is obvious. "C.A.E.", for example, the first variation, is Elgar's wife, Caroline Alice Elgar. Occasionally, the reference is more convoluted. "E.D.U.", for example, the stirring final variation, is Elgar himself. Why E.D.U.? Well, Elgar and Alice often spoke and wrote to each other in a form of intimate, baby language in which Elgar was known not as Edward but "Edoo". Elgar, fond of puns and wordplay, simply made his name into homophonic initials. In some instances, "Dorabella", for example, the variation goes by the name or nickname of the friend, not the initials. Finally, in one instance, Elgar declines to give either initials or a name, referring to the 13th variation as simply:

* * *

Truly enigmatic.

Let's examine the evidence, then, and see if we can't identify all of Elgar's "friends pictured within". On the CD that accompanies this *Friendly Guide,* you will find excerpts from each of the variations, so that you can listen along as you read. All of these excerpts have been taken from a recording made by the Bournemouth Symphony Orchestra, conducted by George Hurst, released on the Naxos label. (Naxos 8.553564).

1 The Original Theme

2 Variation 1: C.A.E.

Who is it? C.A.E. stands for Caroline Alice Elgar. Alice, as she was known, gets pole position in the variations, being the first after the enigmatic original.

What is it like? Almost as melancholic as the theme itself. It starts sounding almost tragic, but soon soon shows its strength. Overall, it suggests Alice is very fondly thought of. There's something of the "domestic goddess" in parts of the variation. It's easy to imagine her as Elgar's own Mrs Beeton.

What did Elgar say about it?

. . . Really a prolongation of the theme, with what I wished to be romantic and delicate additions; those who knew C.A.E. will understand this reference to one whose life was a romantic and delicate inspiration.

3 Variation 2: H.D.S.-P.

Who is it? H.D.S.-P. stands for Hew David Steuart-Powell. As early as the late 1880s, early 1890s, Elgar and Alice would often get together with friends Hew and Basil (Nevinson – see B.G.N.). Elgar, Hew and Basil would play through chamber works, with Hew on piano, Basil on cello and Elgar himself on violin.

What is it like? The soundworld of Variation 2 is heavily influenced by one of Steuart-Powell's practice habits, which was to perform a number of limbering-up, finger exercises, echoes of which can be heard in the music. It's a flibbertigibbety tiny, variation.

What did Elgar say about it?

His characteristic run over the keys before beginning to play is here humorously travestied in the semi-quaver passages . . . chromatic beyond H.D.S.-P.'s liking.

172

4 Variation 3: R.B.T.

Who is it? R.B.T. stands for Richard Baxter Townshend, one of the Elgar's earliest friends. Townshend was married to the sister of Minnie Baker, who was one of Alice's oldest frends, and also, eventually, Dora Penny's stepmother (see Variation 10). Townshend's brother-in-law, therefore, was William Meath Baker (see next variation). What a small world it was, amongst Elgar's friends! As well as an amateur actor, he was also an author, having written, amongst other things, the book *Inspired Golf*, an amusing look at his favourite sport. He is also said to have introduced Elgar to golf. Interestingly enough, the original manuscript copy of this variation is labelled "I.A.", which is usually presumed to have referred to Ivor Atkins, an organist at first Hereford and then Worcester Cathedral. Despite the dedicatee changing between the manuscript and the finished score (why is not known), the music remained the same.

What is it like? Again, a very quirky variation. Quaint sounding, it almost winds itself up, with the theme "birdcalling" above.

What did Elgar say about it?

The variation has a reference to R.B.T.'s presentation of an old man in some amateur theatricals – the low

*voice flying off, occasionally, into "soprano" timbre . . .
the growing grumpiness of the bassoons is important.*

5 Variation 4: W.M.B.

Who is it? W.M.B. stands for William Meath
Baker. He was an almost exact contemporary of
Elgar, but their lives, while linked, were quite
different. Baker was educated at Eton and
Cambridge, inheriting Hasfield Court estate in
Gloucestershire when he was just 18. He was a well-
liked local benefactor who built the Town Hall in
Fenton, now used as a Magistrates Court. Alice and
Elgar called him "The Squire", and his reputation as
a good, if occasionally exacting, host was well
known.

What is it like? Very brusque, almost bombastic-
sounding variation, which seems to forego the
rhythm in the theme and just steamroller it out.

What did Elgar say about it?

*In the days of horses and carriages, it was more
difficult than in these days of petrol to arrange the
carriages for the day to suit a large number of guests.
This variation was written after [Baker] had, with a
slip of paper in his hand, forcibly read out the
arrangements for the day and hurriedly left the music-
room with an inadvertent bang of the door.*

6 Variation 5: R.P.A.

Who is it? R.P.A. stands for Richard Penrose Arnold. He was the son of the poet Matthew Arnold and, like Townshend, a keen amateur golfer who would often join Elgar, Nevinson and others for a round. He was said to have a rather individual laugh, the rhythm of which is imitated in the music.

What is it like? It's exactly like Elgar's comments below, episodic with bouts of dour, low strings, interspersed with flippant, high chattering.

What did Elgar say about it?

His serious conversation was continually broken up by whimsical and witty remarks. [And so] the theme is given by the [double] basses with solemnity, and in the ensuing major portion there is much light-hearted badinage amongst the wind instruments.

7 Variation 6: Ysobel

Who is it? Ysobel is the barely hidden Isobel Fitton who lived in Malvern. She was one of the daughters of Mrs Harriet Fitton, with whom the Elgars often enjoyed musical evenings; their friendship survived until the end of Elgar's life. Although a violin pupil of Elgar's, she was a keen amateur viola player and, so, the variation contains an emotive viola tune.

What is it like? Faltering at first, but grows in confidence as the variation weaves and wends its way along. Suggests a rather complex character.

What did Elgar say about it?

The opening bar, a phrase made use of throughout the variation, is an "exercise" for crossing the strings [*] – a difficulty for beginners; on this is built a pensive and, for a moment, romantic movement.

8 Variation 7: Troyte

Who is it? Troyte was the middle name of Arthur Griffiths. He was a Malvern architect, secretary of the Malvern Concert Club and long-time close friend of Elgar. When Elgar moved into Severn House, in London's Hampstead, it was "Troyte" who redesigned the library to make it more suitable for Elgar's scores and books. His physical appearance – thin and tall – led Elgar to nickname him "Ninepin". "Troyte" himself used to tell friends that this variation was not a musical depiction of him, but of a time when he and Elgar were caught out in a thunderstorm and had to run for cover.

[* The practice of playing a note on one string of the viola followed by a note on the next-but-one. The student had to make sure to avoid playing the string in between.]

What is it like? The boldest variation so far, it fairly marches out of the orchestra, before barking the theme at the audience and retreating. Then . . . it does it all again.

What did Elgar say about it?

The boisterous mood is mere banter. The uncouth rhythm of the drums and lower strings was really suggested by some maladroit essays to play the pianoforte; later the strong rhythm suggests the attempts of the instructor (E.E.) to make something like order out of chaos, and the final despairing "slam" records that the effort proved to be vain.

9 Variation 8: W.N.

Who is it? W.N. stands for Winifred Norbury. She was a close friend whom Elgar met via the Worcestershire Philharmonic Society. She was a close neighbour with the Elgars and accompanied him often, playing piano while he played violin. Interestingly enough, the original sketches bear the label "Secys.", or secretaries: both Winifred Norbury and another woman, Monica Hyde, were secretaries of the Worcestershire Philharmonic Society and some have seen the "Secys." note as meaning that Elgar was intending to encapsulate *both* women in this variation. However, as we'll see below, Elgar himself told an altogether different version of the story. He says it was their house, called Sherridge, near Malvern, that truly informed the music. Nevertheless, it was W.N. who would be commemorated for posterity on the finished score.

What is it like? Again, another fondly observed variation – it brings to mind two "Hinge and Bracket" ladies, perhaps making tea or pruning with secateurs. And of course, W.N.'s last note is Nimrod's first, lending it a little extra glory by association with the Enigma's finest moment.

What did Elgar say about it?

Really suggested by an eighteenth-century house. The gracious personalities of the ladies are sedately shown. W.N. was more connected with music than others of the family, and her initials head the movement; to justify this position a little suggestion of a characteristic laugh is given.

10 Variation 9: Nimrod

Who is it? Nimrod is Elgar's wordplay name for Augustus Johannes Jaeger. Jaeger was a German-born music editor who worked for the publisher, Novello, having moved to England at the age of 18. He worked on all of Elgar's works with Novello from *King Olaf* onwards. Elgar arrived at Nimrod via the fact that "Jäger", in German, means hunter; the "mighty hunter" in the Bible is Nimrod, the

Mesopotamian son of Cush. When Jaeger died in 1908, Elgar wrote of being:

overwhelmed with sorrow for the loss of my dearest and truest friend.

Not surprisingly, Nimrod gets the jewel in the crown of the Enigma Variations, one which, much like Variation 18 in Rachmaninov's *Rhapsody on a Theme of Paganini*, leaves you feeling that you are hearing the very soul, the centrepiece of the work.

What is it like? *Nimrod* has rightly gone on to be one of those pieces of classical music that touches the lives of millions. It is slow, moving, heroic and yet melancholic. As such, it has found a permanent place in the Remembrance Day commemorations around 11 November, each year. One thing to mention, that is not often said about *Nimrod*, is that it is ultimately triumphant, too – the theme appears to win, as it were. Interestingly enough, Elgar re-used Nimrod in his later choral work, *The Music Makers*, a piece in which he "quotes" a number of his own famous tunes, including the *Cello Concerto*.

What did Elgar say about it?

This name is the record of a long summer evening talk, when my friend discoursed eloquently on the slow movements of Beethoven, and said that no one could approach Beethoven at his best in this field, a view with which I cordially concurred . . .... the opening bars are made to suggest the slow movement of the Eighth Sonata (Pathétique). Jaeger was for years the dear friend, the valued adviser and the stern critic of many musicians besides the writer; his place has been occupied but never filled.

11 Variation 10: Dorabella

Who is it? Dorabella is the nickname of Dora Penney, the daughter of the Rector of Wolverhampton. She was said to be a vivacious and lively young woman. She was a frequent companion to Elgar on bicycle rides together, and once cycled 40 miles just to visit him. She was a regular in the Elgar social circles, particularly at Hasfield Court. Elgar took her nickname from one of the character's in the Mozart opera, *Così fan tutte.*

What is it like? Part of the musical character of this movement is said to stem from Dora's stammer, hence the delicate, fluttering strings and flutes, batting the theme to and from one another. Interestingly enough, as most music boffins will tell you, this is not really a variation, in that it has virtually no connection, musically, to the original theme, something Elgar himself pointed out. Also, interestingly enough, Elgar himself once remarked to Dora Penney that she, of all people, should have been able to guess the enigma of the main tune. What did that mean? Furthermore, and also interestingly enough, Dora Penney – or Dora Powell as she became – wrote her own book on Elgar, called "Edward Elgar – Memories of a Variation". Neat title.

What did Elgar say about it?

The pseudonym is adopted from Mozart's "Così fan tutte". The movement suggests a dance-like lightness.

12 Variation 11: G.R.S.

Who is it? G.R.S. stands for George Robertson Sinclair. He was the organist at Hereford Cathedral. Richard Baxter Townshend (the R.B.T. of Variation 3) was his assistant. Sinclair, however, had a pet bulldog named Dan who was often taken on long walks out with his master and the composer. Elgar himself (see below) claimed, then, that it was, in fact, a musical portrait of an incident with the dog, rather than one of its owner.

What is it like? The music does seem to fit a dog more than an owner. There's almost something of the Tom and Jerry about it. Maybe Dan was a bit like like Butch, Tom and Jerry's arch-enemy. Incidentally, Dan's tomb is to be found near the cathedral in Hereford, proudly bearing his birth and death dates.

What did Elgar say about it?

The variation . . . has nothing to do with organs or cathedrals, or, except remotely, with G.R.S. The first few bars were suggested by his great bulldog Dan (a well-known character) falling down the steep bank into the River Wye . . . his paddling upstream to find a landing place . . . and his rejoicing bark on landing . . . G.R.S. said "Set that to music." I did; here it is.

13 Variation 12: B.G.N.

Who is it? B.G.N. stands for Basil Nevinson. He was an amateur cellist introduced to Elgar by Hew David Steuart-Powell, and who, along with Steuart-Powell, made up Elgar's informal chamber trio. Not surprisingly, then, it contains a wonderful solo section for the cello, one in which the subject's seriousness and eloquence is said to shine. Alongside H.D.S.-P., B.G.N. was one of the first variations to be sketched.

What is it like? Naturally, Elgar and the melancholic cello immediately take you to *Cello Concerto* country. Also, because of the cello taking centre-stage, there feels to be more of a connection with the original theme. The combination of the theme and the instrumentation make for a beautifully morose variation.

What did Elgar say about it?

Basil G. Nevinson, an amateur cello player of distinction and the associate with H.D.S.-P. and the writer (violin) in performances of many trios – a serious and devoted friend. The variation is a tribute to a very dear friend whose scientific and artistic attainments, and the whole-hearted way they were put at the disposal of his friends, particularly endeared him to the writer.

14 Variation 13: * * *

Who is it? Three asterisks? Yes, well, this is where another enigma starts. Why did Elgar leave Variation 13 without any name or initials? Could it have been, as some have surmised, simply because it might be unlucky to give anyone the 13th variation? Or could it be something more interesting than that? The movement is, after all, subtitled "Romanza". Well, first of all, let's skip a section and see what Elgar himself had to say about it.

What did Elgar say about it?

The asterisks take the place of the name of a lady who was, at the time of the composition, on a sea voyage. The drums suggest the distant throb of the engines of a liner, over which the clarinet quotes a phrase from Mendelssohn's "Calm Sea and Prosperous Voyage".

183

Interestingly enough, there are at least two possible candidates for this. One is Lady Mary Lygon, a local member of the minor aristocracy. Although she wasn't a very close friend of the Elgars, she did sail to Australia around the time of the writing or publication of the *Enigma Variations*. (Oddly enough, though, she wasn't at sea when Elgar says his "***" was. Was he just remembering wrongly or deliberately trying to put people off the scent?) The second possibility is Helen Weaver, a woman who had been Elgar's fiancée for just 18 months in 1883/84. The engagement was broken off – inexplicably, whereupon Helen Weaver emigrated to New Zealand in 1885. She married an Auckland bank manager five years later.

What is it like? An interesting blend of sounds, really. If this IS the love of Elgar's life, then it doesn't feel like it – there are much fonder movements. Admittedly it has "bereft" moments, but it's hard to see that this might be "the one", as it were. He uses a method called coin drumming to possibly evoke the "absent friend" – coins are literally placed on the timpani in order to add an extra resonance to the drumming.

15 Variation 14: E.D.U.

Who is it? E.D.U. stands for Edoo, Elgar himself (Edoo was Alice's pet name for the composer).

What is it like? A lively, bracing movement that roughs and tumbles its way to the end, rounding the entire work off with a bang, and incorporating references to Alice's variation and *Nimrod* too. It suggests that Elgar was saying: "You just wait, you unbelievers . . . I'll show you what I can do!" It's a real showcase for all his talents, in one variation.

What did Elgar say about it?

Written at a time when friends were dubious and generally discouraging as to the composer's musical future, this variation is merely to show what E.D.U. (a paraphrase of a fond name) intended to do. References made to Var. I (C.A.E.) and to Var. IX (Nimrod), two great influences on the life and art of the composer, are entirely fitting to the intention of the piece. The whole of the work is summed up in the triumphant, broad presentation of the theme in the major.

The Enigma of the Hidden Tune

When Elgar wrote the *Enigma Variations*, at the end of 1898 and the beginning of 1899, he created a mystery which was the Da Vinci Code of its day.

Initially, Elgar didn't say anything about the main tune of the *Enigma Variations*, certainly not in terms of a mystery. While composing it, he remarked that each movement was in the style of a friend, but, at the outset, that was as far as the mystery went.

Elgar first "spoke" on the subject when asked for information for the concert programme notes. Then, he went on record as saying that he would not explain "The Enigma", and that he would not divulge its "dark saying". He then went on to add another layer of mystery. Across the whole set of variations, another bigger theme "goes but is not played. So the principal theme never appears . . ." This, he said, was the equivalent of a play where a character was often referred to throughout but was never actually seen.

Privately, Elgar intimated that the "hidden theme" was a well-known tune. Also, oddly enough, he later stated that the main theme was himself – indeed, he was known to have signed himself in letters, not with a signature, but with the first four notes of the *Enigma Variations'* main tune.

So, the "enigma" of the *Enigma Variations*, it seemed, worked on several levels.

First, the individual enigmas of each movement, working out the initials or names given to each movement and matching them to their subject.

Second, the enigma of the three asterisks of the 13th variation. To whom do they refer and why did Elgar feel he couldn't apply the subject's name or initials to the music?

Finally, and most intriguingly, the enigma of the missing tune itself. As the first two parts have been dealt with above, let's look at the third.

Over the years, the idea that Elgar wrote his main tune to the *Enigma Variations* as a counter-melody to another famous tune, which is left unplayed, has exercised some of the greatest musical brains. In fact, some refuse to believe there *is* any hidden tune, pointing to the fact that Elgar said there was another "theme" that goes unplayed – not "tune". Maybe, they say, there is no tune at all. Maybe Elgar meant a philosophical theme – the most popular suggestion put forward is that the theme is the loneliness and ever-present melancholy of the composer himself.

But if the "theme" were a tune, which ones are the main contenders? Over the years, many have been put forward, ranging from the sublime to the ridiculous. A brief list of some of them follows, as well as our very own, highly personal view on their suitability, plus an Estimated Likelihood Grading and Rating number – our ELGaR factor.

Contenders for the "theme"

Possible tune	Comments	ELGaR factor
"*Auld Lang Syne*"	One of the most popular candidates over the years. Has even been studied for its suitability by the best musical brains – which might make you stop and think the next time you lock arms on New Year's Eve. In the end, scores low in our ELGaR factor because of the fact that it would only fit over a tiny amount of the tune, leaving most of the Engima theme blank – so not really the "larger" tune to which Elgar referred, surely? Having said that, it was said that his friend, Dora Penney's, insistence that this was the hidden theme is what led Elgar to break off their friendship. Was he niggled that somebody was getting too close?	5 / 10
"*God Save the Queen*"	Again, not very likely. Why? Well, only fits over a part of the tune, again, and sometimes not perfectly – surely Elgar would have fitted his mystery tune correctly? Also, has to be in the major key (happier, brighter sounding) while the "Enigma" theme is in the minor (sad, more melancholy-sounding)	3 / 10
"*Home Sweet Home*"	Do people really suggest this might be it? Well, yes they do, even though it a) is too short, and b) doesn't really even fit A no hoper in our book	1 / 10
"*Rule Britannia*"	This became a candidate as late as the 1970s (yes, they really are still trying). Too many clashes with the Enigma tune, though, for our liking	4 / 10

Mozart's *Prague Symphony*	This is often suggested as being a tune that Elgar used as a starting point for his. Relying on the repeated nature of Mozart's tune, it can be shown to bear some resemblance. Also, the fact that the *Prague Symphony* was included in the same concert at which the *Enigma Variations* was premiered adds a little frisson	3 / 10
The "*Dies Irae*" tune	Used in many requiems, this tune, as fitting in melancholy spirit as it might be, doesn't really fit	2 / 10
Beethoven's *Pathétique Sonata*	Again, like the Mozart, often considered a possible starting point for Elgar, largely because of the resemblance to the tune. We're not sure, though	3 / 10

Bearing in mind that the mystery of the *Enigma Variations* is now 108 years old, and that Elgar himself took the secret of his hidden tune to his grave, we would be foolish to pitch ourselves against more than a century of the world's best musical thinkers in trying to identify the "Enigma" tune. And yet . . ..

Well, one comment Elgar made to Dora Penney has always intrigued. He told her: "You of all people should be able to figure out what the missing tune was." Many have wondered if that had something to do with a play on her last name – Penney. Maybe . . . Beethoven's *Rage over a Lost Penny*? Here, we think it might just have been a reference to her other name – Dorabella, the nickname Elgar gave her. Where did he take this nickname from? From Mozart's opera, *Così fan tutte*.

So, if you fancy trying to solve the mystery of the *Enigma Variations*, we suggest you start at *Così fan tutte*. Now there's a challenge.

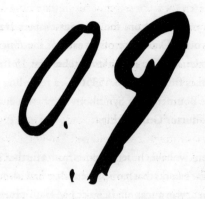

Have a Listen Yourself. Part 2: Further Listening

As usual in our *Classic FM Friendly Guides*, we have included a CD of classical music extracts. These short excerpts are designed to whet your appetite to discover for yourself more of Elgar's music.

Each of our choices has been taken from the Naxos label, which offers a wide range of excellent recordings at a budget price. Hopefully, this will encourage you to sample Elgar's music without too much risk to your wallet or purse. As well as being released on CD, all of these works are available to download in full on our website, **www.classicfm.com/downloads**.

As you know from the previous chapter, tracks 1–15 on our CD are excerpts of each of the *Enigma Variations*. The music from these first 15 tracks comes from Naxos 8.553564 – a recording made by the Bournemouth Symphony Orchestra and the conductor George Hurst.

Here, we have chosen excerpts from a further 10 of Elgar's works that have proven popular with our listeners in our annual Classic FM Hall of Fame Countdown.

16 Cello Concerto in E minor

Melancholic, certainly. But extraordinarily moving as well. We like to think that it captures something of the beauty of the English countryside, being written, as it was, at Brinkwells, deep in the Sussex countryside.

This is an excerpt taken from Naxos 8.554409.

17 Chanson de Matin

This is one of a pair of pieces that bookend the day. Its partner work is *Chanson de Nuit*. Whereas *Chanson de Matin* is lively and bright, *Chanson de Nuit* is a rather more dark affair.

This is an excerpt taken from Naxos 8.554166.

18 Serenade for Strings

When you listen to this wonderful piece, it's hard to believe that Elgar's publishers initially turned it down. What on earth could they have been thinking? This was one of those works that owed a lot to Alice's influence over her husband.

This is an excerpt taken from Naxos 8.550331.

19 Pomp and Circumstance March No. 4

We think that you're almost certainly familiar with Elgar's *Pomp and Circumstance March No. 1*, which features the tune *"Land of Hope and Glory"*, so we have chosen the fourth in this series of five marches. It's not quite as popular as the first, but it's still a rollicking good listen.

This is an excerpt taken from Naxos 8.554161.

20 Salut d'Amour

This is one of those pieces of music that is able to conjure up a particular moment and a particular place in history. Close your eyes and think of Victorian England, before the ravages of the First World War took their toll.

This is an excerpt taken from Naxos 8.550306.

21 Imperial March

Another of those patriotic pieces that made Elgar famous, this was penned for Queen Victoria's Diamond Jubilee. It was given its premiere at the Crystal Palace in 1897.

This is an excerpt taken from Naxos 8.550634.

22 Symphony No. 1 in A Flat

It took Elgar an awfully long time to get around to writing his first symphony – but it was worth the wait. His great pal, Hans Richter, told the LSO, as they were about to begin their rehearsal:

Gentlemen, let us now rehearse the greatest symphony of modern times written by the greatest modern composer – and not only in this country!

This is an excerpt taken from Naxos 8.550634.

23 The Dream of Gerontius

Based on a text by Cardinal Newman, this was one of Elgar's greatest choral works. For the story of the work, see page 49.

This is an excerpt taken from Naxos 8.553885-86.

24 Violin Concerto

This is not an easy piece for the soloist to play, but perhaps that is because Elgar was himself a violinist. He knew just how far the instrument could be pushed in technical terms. He dedicated the work to the great violinist Fritz Kreisler.

This is an excerpt taken from Naxos 8.553233.

25 Cockaigne Overture

We finish our selection of extracts from Elgar's greatest works with an overture. Despite appearances, the name of this work has nothing whatsoever to do with Class A drugs and is instead taken from an old nickname for London. (It's where we get the term Cockney from.) The *Cockaigne Overture* is sometimes given the subtitle *"In London Town"*. It's great fun!

This is an excerpt taken from Naxos 8.550489.

Elgar's Movie Music

You may well have already been an Elgar fan when you picked up this book, but if you were new to the man and his music, we hope that we have persuaded you of his greatness by now.

It's now time for you to take up the baton and to proselytize about his great work. One of the easiest ways of persuading a non-classical music listener to give it a try is through the cinema.

There are two sorts of music used in the movies: film soundtracks by composers such as John Williams, James Horner, Howard Shore and Hans

Zimmer; or pieces of classical music borrowed by the film director because they create the appropriate sound to accompany the pictures on the screen.

Elgar's music has not been used as often in movies as that of some other popular composers, and you will notice that the film directors' choices centre around a few key pieces of music. Nevertheless, here is a list of his works to listen out for when you're next watching the relevant DVD:

Brassed Off: *Pomp and Circumstance March No. 1*
Children of the Marshland: *Nimrod* from *Enigma Variations*
A Clockwork Orange: *Pomp and Circumstance March No. 1*
Crush: *Nimrod* from *Enigma Variations*
Elizabeth: *Nimrod* from *Enigma Variations*
Fantasia 2000: *Pomp and Circumstance Marches Nos. 1 & 4*
Greystoke: The Legend of Tarzan, Lord of the Apes: *Pomp and Circumstance March No. 4* and *Symphony No. 1*
Hilary and Jackie: *Cello Concerto*
If Looks Could Kill: *Pomp and Circumstance March No. 1*
A Judgement in Stone: *Cello Concerto*
Lorenzo's Oil: *Cello Concerto*
Mrs. Miniver: *Pomp and Circumstance March No. 1*
Reality Bites: *Pomp and Circumstance March No. 1*

You might also like to get hold of a copy of the director Ken Russell's documentary film, which is simply called "Elgar". It is now widely available on DVD.

Where to Find Out More

As we said in the introduction to this book, our *Friendly Guide* is not intended to be the definitive work on Elgar's life and music. Instead, we hope that it has helped to fire up your interest in the great man.

There are some very fine books available that will help you on your journey of discovery into all things Elgar. In our view, the very finest of these is *The Life of Elgar* by the incomparable Michael Kennedy (published by Cambridge University Press). Other excellent biographies include *Elgar* by Simon Mundy (published by Omnibus Press) and

Elgar, "Enigma Variations" by Julian Rushton (published by Cambridge University Press).

You will find a wealth of information and analysis in *The Cambridge Companion to Elgar* by Daniel M. Grimley and Julian Rushton (published by Cambridge University Press). For a really detailed understanding of what made Elgar tick, you should take a look at *Edward Elgar: A Creative Life* by the great Elgar scholar Jerrold Northrop Moore (published by Clarenden Paperbacks). This is a mighty work, running to some 858 pages. The same author has produced another fascinating book, *Elgar: Child of Dream* (published by Faber & Faber), which looks at the themes behind Elgar's music.

If you find yourself becoming a real Elgar fan, then you should have no doubt about becoming a member of the Elgar Society. This excellent organization is dedicated to ensuring that the memory of Elgar and his music lives on well into the 21st century – and beyond. Full details can be found on the society's website, **www.elgar.org.uk**. It's also packed with biographical information.

You really should also visit the Elgar Birthplace Museum, just outside Worcester. It was set up by Elgar's daughter, Carice, in 1934, with a new Elgar Centre added in 2000. For more information, check out their website at **www.elgarfoundation.org.**

In terms of more general guides to classical music, we hope that you would enjoy one of the other books in this series, *The Classic FM Friendly Guide to Music* by Darren Henley, also published by Hodder Arnold, which is the basis for Tony Robinson's highly successful Classic FM radio series of the same name. The *DK Eyewitness Companion to Classical Music*, edited by John Burrows (published by Dorling Kindersley), is a very colourful and reliable source of information on the chronology of classical music. For a slightly quirkier walk through the subject, we recommend *Stephen Fry's Incomplete & Utter History of Classical Music*, which is published by Macmillan and is based on the eponymous Classic FM radio series, written by Tim Lihoreau. We also hope that you enjoy the Classic FM book *Classic Ephemera* by Darren Henley and Tim Lihoreau (published by Boosey & Hawkes), which is packed full of classical music facts, stories and trivia.

For younger classical music lovers or discoverers, *The Story of Classical Music* and *Famous Composers, Volumes 1 & 2* are published by Naxos Audiobooks, in association with Classic FM. These titles are aimed at 8–14-year-olds and contain musical excerpts and CD-ROM elements.

For up-to-the-minute news on the latest CD releases of Elgar's music, *Classic FM Magazine* is an excellent source, with around 150 reviews each month. You might also enjoy reading *The Gramophone,* the magazine that many music enthusiasts regard as the last word in classical music criticism.

Elgar's music features very heavily on Classic FM. We broadcast 24 hours a day across the UK on 100 – 102 FM, and also on DAB Digital Radio and through digital satellite and cable television. You can also listen online at **www.classicfm.com.**

If you have yet to hear Elgar's compositions performed live, then you really should. We believe that there is simply no substitute for hearing classical music in the flesh, so to speak. Classic FM has a series of partnerships with orchestras across the country: the Royal Scottish National Orchestra, the Royal Liverpool Philharmonic Orchestra, the Philharmonia Orchestra and the London Symphony Orchestra. To see if they have an Elgar concert coming up somewhere near you, log on to **www.classicfm.com** and click on the "Concerts and Events" section.

Happy listening!

Elgar Mood Chart

Dead Calm	Steady as she goes	Picking up	Flag waving	Red Hot

Nimrod --

Symphony No. 1 --------------

Salut d'Amour -------------

"Where Corals Lie" (Sea Pictures)   Variation 14 (Enigma)

-------- Chanson de Matin --------

------- Ave Verum ------   Cockaigne Overture ----------------

-------- Serenade for Strings --------   -- Demons' Chorus ----
(Dream of Gerontius)

-------- Symphony No. 2 --------   Froissart -------

--------------- Violin Concerto ------------

Pomp and Circumstance March No. 2

Nursery Suite --------   ------Introduction & Allegro for Strings --------

Sospiri   ------- Cello Concerto (First Movement) ----------------

203

Index

About the Authors

Tim Lihoreau is the Creative Director of Classic
FM and of the new national digital radio station,
theJazz. He studied music at the University of Leeds
and worked as a professional pianist and in the
record industry, before joining Jazz FM's music
team in 1990. He moved to Classic FM in 1993.
Since then, he has been responsible for writing and
producing many of Classic FM's most acclaimed
programmes, in the process winning more awards
than any other producer or presenter in the station's
history. He has been honoured by the Sony Radio
Academy Awards, the Arqiva Commercial Radio
Awards and the New York International Radio
Festival. He has written regularly for the *Daily
Telegraph*, the *Independent* and *Classic FM*

Magazine. His books include *Stephen Fry's Incomplete & Utter History of Classical Music*, published by Macmillan. His humorous writings away from classical music include the best-selling book *Modern Phobias*, published by Bloomsbury.

Darren Henley has worked at Classic FM since 1992, becoming Managing Editor in 2000, Station Manager in 2004 and Managing Director of Classic FM and theJazz in 2006. He has written, edited or contributed to 16 books about classical music and musicians. He began his career as a journalist at Invicta Radio in Kent and then at ITN. His radio programmes have been honoured by the Sony Radio Academy Awards, the British Radio Awards, the New York International Radio Festival and the United Nations. Two of his audiobooks for children, *The Story of Classical Music* and *Famous Composers*, were consecutively named as best original work by the American Audiobook Publishers Association in 2005 and 2006. Both are published by Naxos Audiobooks. *The Story of Classical Music* also won the *Radio Times* Readers' Choice Award at the British Spoken Word Awards in 2005 and was nominated for a Grammy Award.

The Classic FM Friendly Guide to Elgar is the seventh book about classical music that Tim Lihoreau and Darren Henley have written together.